# HEALTH & ASTROLOGY

# HEALTH
# &
# ASTROLOGY

*By*

**B.K. CHATURVEDI**

**GOODWILL PUBLISHING HOUSE**
**B-3, RATTAN JYOTI, 18, RAJENDRA PLACE**
**NEW DELHI-110008 (INDIA)**

Published by
**Rajneesh Chowdhry**
*for*
**Goodwill Publishing House**
B-3, Rattan Jyoti
18, Rajendra Place
New Delhi-110008
Tel. : 5750801, 5755519
Fax : 91-11-5763428

*Typeset at*
Radha Laserkraft
R-814, New Rajinder Nagar
New Delhi-110060 • Tel. : 5730031

*Printed at  Kumar Offset Printers, Delhi-110 031*

# *Preface*

It gives the author immense pleasure to present this work "Health And Astrology" before our discerning readership. Although there are many books available which deal with this topic, not many are available that discuss the topic elaborately and exclusively in one volume. Special emphasis has also been laid on those dreaded diseases like AIDS and Cancer whose astrological connotations have been analysed so threadbare along with remedial measures. It is believed that a judicious blend of medical cum-astrological remedial measures will help the distressed get relieved of the affliction at a faster pace.

One word about exclusion of the trans-saturnine planets like Neptune, Herchel and Pluto. Since it is believed that the Nodal points viz. Rahu and Ketu account for all other heavenly effects — as is rightly believed by the traditional school of Indian astrology — they have not been included in this study though their effect through the nodal points have been taken into consideration. Various ready-reckoner charts for the identification of the diseases and their area of pin-pointed consideration have also been added to help the readers in their easy identification. A separate chapter has also been added to determine the possible way of one's meeting, one's end to make this study truly comprehensive as the fact cannot be denied that no matter what we do death can't be defied which is an inevitable consequence of life. The Dasha system has also been given a glimpse of for the convenience of the reader.

Lastly, the author wants to share with his readers his gratitude to his elder brother, M.N. Chaturvedi, and nephew, Gaurav Chaturvedi, whose open minded analysis helped the author a lot in compiling and interpreting various planets' astro-medical significance. The author is also very much grateful to Mr. Rajneesh Chaudhari of "Goodwill Publications" who provided all the help in quite a liberal measure to prepare this book of a unique kind. May they all live long ! If this book could help in relieving the afflictions of even one person, the author would feel that his labour has been duly rewarded. He is sure that this book may not make them happier but it would not leave our readers sadder than before. It is hoped that this would receive as warm a welcome as was accorded by our discerning readership to 'Love and Astrology'.

— **B.K. CHATURVEDI**

# Contents

## A PRAYER

*May I have breath in my nostrils;*
*Voice in my mouth;*
*Sight in my eyes;*
*Hearing in my ears;*
*Hair that has not turned grey;*
*Teeth that are not discoloured;*
*And much strength in my arms.*
*May I have power in my thighs;*
*Swiftness in my legs;*
*Steadfastness in my feet !*
*May all my limbs remain unimpaired*
*And my soul (Atma) unconquered !*

—RIGVEDA

# CHAPTER ONE

# Planets and Health

That the plants influence the life on earth is too established a fact to need further elaboration. And if the planets show their effect on human body naturally they must also be casting their effect on the three basic humours that govern the health of a body. Although these radiations affect all beings we shall be confining our study to human beings only.

Health is of vital significance in human life. No matter how great thinker or scholar one may be, using the Shakespearean jargon, it can be reaffirmed that "there is yet to be a great philosopher who could bear toothache patiently !" But unfortunately, not much attention has been paid to astrology's application in keeping one's health good. Although in India in the matrimonial fields astrological considerations, matching horoscopes and propitiating various adverse planets etc. have remained indispensable for many millennia yet in the field of health not much use astrology has been put to. Whereas, the fact is that astrology can be as useful in this field as medical science could be. Like your doctor advising you to be cautious about your doing physical exertion when your blood pressure is high, the same way when you are passing through the transit effect of some adverse planet or adverse Mahadasha (Major period) you should hold back making important decisions or launching some new projects. In health region, refrain from showing temper when Mars is adversely placed or Saturn is casting adverse aspect. Although every day we see in newspapers, periodicals or even TV shows displaying the planetary effect for particular sign on a any particular day, such forecasts are too general to be given any individual attention to. If India's population is roughly taken to be 1 billion, the prediction for each sign among

1

all the 12 signs of the Zodiac can not be true and meaningful to more than 80 million people ! But surprisingly, people feel drawn towards those general predictions even without the realisation that they have no significance for an individual. Moreover, the language of the predictions is deliberately held to be so ambiguous and general as to leave almost an infinite scope for personal interpretation. Also, the authors of these predictions are such deft persons as to write them with finesse that they cannot be interpreted wrongly either ! Suppose it is written that 'this week you might keep an indifferent health.' The concerned sign's native would interpret even his casual sneezing as to mark of his indifferent health. Even then it can't be held that people don't pay attention to astrological consideration concerning their health and well being.

It is to bring them on to the right track and tell them that astrology could be very useful in helping them keep their health good that this book was thought of. This book will tell you that if you have the Moon afflicted, you might remain susceptible to cold throughout your life; that an adverse Mars is likely to make your blood pressure fluctuate quite frequently or adverse Saturn's position accentuated by adverse Rahu may weaken your nerves. Although the remedial measures will also be suggested liberally yet the basic 'manufacturing defects' will have to be given extra attention to.

As a matter of fact, throughout the centuries, astrology had close connections with medicine. In ancient India astrology and Ayurveda were intimately connected. An Ayurvedic doctor (or Vaidya) was required to be an astrologer too. But with the introduction of allopathy into India, the importance of astrology as a diagnostic test was reduced for a time. However, now a reaction appears to be gradually setting in largely due to the fact that even the leading medical men in the west have started recognising astrology's diagnostic importance.

The dependency between the Sun and disease-incidence has been recognised in India for ages. Apart from wave-radiation, the Sun also sends off flows of corpuscles which are sometimes dabbed "the solar wind". Instruments installed on artificial satellites and rockets have shown that corpuscular radiation prevents flown of plasma which have magnetic fields of their own. This magnetic field interacts with the magnetic field of the earth and influences terrestrial phenomena.

2

It can affect the electrical potential of an individual including the electrical activity of the brain.[1] Dry to this electric activity, various nerves impulses are sorted out and converted into sensation, thoughts and actions. It will be seen that it is the geometrical arrangements of planets-that give rise to solar flares. In astrological language, these planetary arrangements are called the 'Yogas' which denote definite pattern of events. As has been conclusively proved, human beings have around them an energy shed or field, which corresponds to the had around the radio active particles. With varied intensity the body radiates with different organs. Therefore its health or ill-health depends upon the harmony existing between its radiation and the intensity of radiations received from the Sun, as well as from cosmos at a given time. In simpler language it can be said that certain influences are exerted on our bodies by planets and stars and there are tendencies which can be dealt with by human being in a positive or negative manner. According to the modern researches, there is considerable voltage increase in the electrical potential of a human being between the time of New Moon and Full Moon. These electrical changes correspond with sharp changes in the person's moods. Consequently the forces behind the Moon are said to aggravate maladjustments and conflicts.

In fact the modern gynaecologists deserve to pay greater attention to the writings on NISHEKAVIDHI which elaborately dilates upon the ideas concerning the periodic fertility in a woman and their correlation to certain cosmic patterns. It is believed that the best fertile periods for conception in women (in the case of 28 and 30 days of menstrual cycles) are the 14th, 15th and 16th days from the commencement of menstruation. And according to the astrological work 'JATAKA PARIJATA', the nights of 14, 15 and 16 are the best for concerning offspring.

At this juncture a reference to the famous theory of 'Tri-Dosha' appears quite apt. As commonly understood, vata, pitta and kapha or Sleshma are taken to mean gas, bile and phlegm respectively. The word 'vata' is derived from the root 'Va', meaning motion or indicative of motion. The word 'pitta' has its root in 'tapa' meaning

---

[1] It has been proved by medical researches that the human brain, radiates into surrounding space electromagnetic energy in the form of radio-waves.

3

agitation, excitation or energy while 'kapha' or Shleshma means clasp, attraction, embrace, gravitation or that which joins or clasps'. Put in a different way, these three qualities correspond to motion, energy and inertia. Thus it may be erroneous to assume that 'vata', 'pitta' and 'kapha' are just the three chemical substances of wind, bile and mucus. As the great Sushruta says, just as the Sun, the Moon and wind are necessary for the regular functioning of this world, so also it is 'vata, pitta and kapha that regulate the health of the human body'. The effect of the three physical qualities (motion, energy and gravitation or inertia) on the living cell on the same lines as it is in the cosmos.

The human ailments, thus, could be linked to the outcome of the gravitational pull exerted by planets through rotation and revolution. The disequilibrium that arises in the 'Doshas' are due to attraction between the field-forces emanating from the planets on one side and the human organism on the other.

According to the Indian school of astrology, there are three groups of asterism which are in line with the three doshas of Ayurveda. For instance one born in a 'vata' group of constellations would indeed be generally predisposed towards diseases and signs have also governance over three 'dhatus'. The Sun governs mostly pitta and a little of 'vata', the Moon mostly vata etc. In the astrological interpretations explained ahead, there is a thorough clarification of diseases and the planetary patterns which cause them.

Astrology believes that the Moon rules the mind, the Sun rules the soul or self and Mercury rules the nervous system. Disorders arising from psychosis and neurosis and certain mental abnormalities-exaggeration of certain traits recognisable nearly in all people are respectively caused by combination of factors involving the Moon, Mercury, Mars, Saturn and the Nodes (Rahu and Ketu).

A recent research has also discovered a marked correspondence between different types of mental disorders and Mercury's affliction. This conforms with the old aphorism that if in a horoscope, the Moon and Mercury are in a certain mutual dispositions afflicted by Mars, Saturn or the Nodes, it generally indicates mental disorders.

In actual practice such a combination is present mostly in the horoscopes of person suffering from obsessional neurosis, delusions

4

and false belief. The declination of Mercury can give clues as to whether a person's 'escape mechanism' will make him brood over the past, or hug the illusion of a fool's paradise in the present, or get into utopia of the future. But a Jupiterean aspect will change the picture entirely. Then the person will be thoughtful and will have a very understanding mind and good power of judgement. In case the Moon is removed and substituted by Mars and the nature develops mechanical aptitude. If one is suffering from mental fatigue, enhanced self-consciousness, development of an inferiority complex, general irritability, deep seated fear, one can predict that he has the Moon and Rahu in conjunction aspected by Saturn. If instead of the Moon, the affliction is centred on the Ascendant, the symptoms reveal themselves in the form of fatigue, eye tremour, nausea, soreness of the muscles, etc. Melancholia is produced by the simple conjunction of the Moon and Saturn. Such a person suffers from acute depression. Of course, constellational positions modify the effects. The Sun-Jupiter-Mars influences centred on Mercury or the Moon induce the neurotic disease called schizophrenia. If the ruling planet happens to be that of Mars the native is prone to develop a persecution complex. Studies in astropsycology have revealed interesting details as regards the positive and negative traits of planets. On the positive side, the moon is imaginative and variable. On the negative side irresponsible, moody and vacillating. Saturn is conscientious, clear headed, careful, self controlled and conservatively conscious. On the negative side, be is narrow minded fixated, callous, miserly and ambitions in a selfish way.

Similarly, Rahu, on the positive side is rather unconventional, independent and humanistic. On the negative side, he is unsocial, eccentric, neurotic and mildly destructive. The interpretation of these traits depends upon the experience and knowledge of the psycho-astrologer.

The science of medical astrology deals with innumerable diseases. Diseases like consumption, blindness, hysteria, menstrual disorders, leprosy, rheumatism, gastric troubles, cardiac troubles etc. have been dealt with extensively. No doubt the medical science with its improvements, x-ray, blood-tests etc. has made great strides towards better methods of diagnosis, but the modern physicians must try to make difference between bookish knowledge and actual knowledge acquired through practical experience. The physician's role is to discover the characteristics of the sick man's individuality, his resistance to pathogenic factors, his sensibility to pain, his innate traits and individuality. This individual should be 'revealed' by the analysis of the probabilities of organic, humoral and psychological personality which can also be revealed to greater degree of precision by an organised study of the horoscope. The horoscope can also show the latent tendencies to diseases. When the planetary aspects have been stirred into action, the Dasha (period), Antardasha (sub period) or Antardasha[1] can give the diagnostician the key to it. The electrocardiographs, the EEG etc. and measuring the metabolism rate are useful but not enough. There are not merely two types of metabolism but in reality 12 different types to which the only clue can be supplied by organised astrological reality. Thus the Sun, when in Taurus and receiving the rays of Saturn, is tumour-forming. Or when Saturn is in Aquarius and affects the Sun or the Moon the native is likely become nervous and jittery, has undue perspiration. There are also conditions not recognised in medicine which, none-the-less, markedly interfere with health. Those who have the Sun and the Moon in the fiery signs or constellations are subject to the condition which, while not a disease, can have very detrimental results if not corrected. They tend to become dehydrated and if they live in a dry, warm and sunny climate will develop a nervous state almost impossible to diagnose.

The extra ordinary insight in medical astrology helps the doctor get a peep into the nature of the entire personality of the patient. That is why this book may help you even knowing your strong points and shortcomings. You may know your level of vitality. It won't be incongruous to point that the position of the Sun is of the greatest consequence in understanding the vitality of the person. The cause of variation in solar-radiation intensities at the surface of the earth are the orbital distance between the Sun and the earth. In July, when the Sun is in the Cancer, for instance, the distance between the Sun and the earth is greatest. During this period, the biological energy waxes in the northern hemisphere and biological activity takes on a new

---

[1]Minor Sub Period.

pattern. In January (when the Sun is in Capricorn), he is nearest to the earth and the radiation-intensity exceeds by 7%. The horoscope is cast, taking the longitude and latitude of the place of birth, when the angular, solar, and planetary positions affect animate and inanimate things. Astrologically, one who has Cancer rising, will have low vitality and he is too loath to follow the advice of others. He is suspicious by nature and lacks faith in others. But when the Sun is in this sign, the native has more vitality. Cancer has the rule over stomach, diaphragm, upper lobes of the liver, the pancreas and the gastrio vein and serum of the blood. Although the opinion might vary over the actual hold of a particular sign over human body it can't be denied that the 12 signs of the zodiac do have their well defined positions over the human body. We shall be elaborating over these topics in the chapters ahead, but suffice it to say here that if astrology is considered as a side-help in medical diagnosis, it shall all the more ease the doctor's job in identifying the root cause of any illness. It is perhaps for this precise reason that the ancient yet still vibrant school of medicine, the Ayurveda pays great emphasis on the 'mool-prakrit' or the basic nature of the person.

The horoscope can construct a fairly accurate picture of the individuals psyche his temperament, his likes and dislikes, aptitudes, his moods, his abilities and weaknesses and strong traits. For instance, it is said that one born when the distance between the Sun and the Moon is 12° will be "Vyasanakta chittascha', i.e. 'given to worrying'. This information can usually supplement the diagnosis of normal psychology arrived at by its vocational tests, its intelligence and other characters of various kinds. It can help educational institutions in guiding students in the choice of careers. It can help industry of making the most of the different types of workers in giving them jobs suitable to their temperaments. Above all it can help the individual to guide his plans and career to suit his character traits, avoid lines in which he has no flair and take up lines in which he has a natural aptitude. Astrology reveals the general tendencies inherent in certain types of persons by reason of the positions of the planets and stars at their birth. We can use them in the art of life and make the best of our endowment.

This way, as is apparent, astrology can be of immense help to let is stay healthy and successful. So consulting your doctor and the astrologer is as necessary as your getting education. Of course astrology won't be able to ward off the diseases that your body is most likely susceptible to fall victim of but this can also suggest the pre-emptive remedial measure. An analogy can be given. No matter how advance to your computer in meteorological department you can't prevent the rains. But certainly an advance knowledge of the weather can guard you to leave your home with the umbrella or raincoat to escape the inconvenience likely to be caused by rain. Like a diabetic taking insulin infection to check the rise in blood sugar level, you can wear a coral to check the disturbance to be caused in your life by a bad Mars.

There are some rationalist who question the very efficiency of these remedial measures with the argument that these far off planets can hardly influence our life on the earth. But how would they explain the real pearl casting extra glow on the full moon night even if that gem may be kept in a dark and dinghy corner ? Also, how do the planetary movements through various constellations ascertain the measure of rainfall ? Why the medical researches all over the world confirm the incidence of lunatic disorders most on the full moon day ? After all, if the full moon can cause high tide in the oceans how it can spare the human body having most of the fluids guiding its activities ? All these explanations do provide a solid base to treat astrology a science. After all, what is science ? That which is based on logical reasoning, empirical observations, theoretical deductions arrived at impartially. Based on observation and reasoning the results are obtained with precise calculations. Like a pale figure, by simple observation may tend to guide a medical practitioner to respect anaemia, similarly an afflicted Mars may guide the astrologer to predict blood-related complication. Those who doubt the scientific base of astrology on account of its predictions' occasional failure provide themselves a strong argument for astrology to be treated as an exact science. It requires not only expert knowledge of the basic principles of astrology but also an overall insight into horoscopic chart coupled with situation to arrive at correct astrological prediction. Moreover, it is a science which requires its learners to bear a high normal stature and an impartial vision. Like a greedy engineer may lead to a collapse of a dam whose construction is entrusted to him or a doctor in the lure of money may cheat his patient and lead him to greater harm, an incompetent astrologer may also bring blot to the visage of this fairly accurate science. In order to escape them quacks sullying this science what should be done is having authorised institutions to impart this knowledge. Nevertheless this discussion is beyond the scope of this book. So we would end this debate asserting that astrology is a science whose advantage should be taken as fruitfully as one seeks help from a registered physician.

As the coming pages will reveal, the empirical experience of many nullennia has proved the veracity of this branch of knowledge. Particularly in the sphere of human health, an organised astrological study can provide a great help to ensure one's good health. It, though, is quite platitudinous to say that health is vital for life yet the fact can't be denied that all good 'Raj-yogas' or 'kirti-yogas' become meaningless if one is not ensured of a good health. No doubt a powerful Saturn might bestow upon you a powerful 'Raja-Zoga' but of what significance will that be if you are bed-ridden or too weak to enjoy that glorious period ? It is after considering this vital fact that this book has been devised.

Since people have scanty or insufficient knowledge to understand the astrological interpretation in general, the chapter coming ahead tells you about the basics of astrology to enable you follow all that explained in the coming chapters.

# CHAPTER TWO

# The Basics of Astrology

**Note.** In case you are versed in the terminology of astrology, you can easily skip this chapter. But if you want to learn what future holds for you in the matters of health without any ambiguity, this chapter may prove very useful to you.

It is an ancient belief of almost all civilisations that heavenly bodies do cast their influence on life on earth. If the primitive man found himself to be more energetic with the rising sun and rather lethargic and romantic with the moon shooting up in the sky, he became convinced that these luminaries have their impact upon his life. This led to his selecting and identifying certain 'stars' in the sky which seemed to have lasting effect upon his life. He also detected the negative influence of these heavenly bodies and learnt by experience as to how they could be propitiated. Identifying them as the minor deities he began to worship them with great devotion. The Navagrahas or nine planets that the subsequent findings selected are called 'graha' which literally means the one that grasps you or whose influence possesses you. These are the following:

SUN, MOON, MARS, MERCURY, JUPITER, VENUS, SATURN, RAHU and KETU.

Although other 'latest' planets like, URANUS, NEPTUNE, PLUTO, HERCHEL etc. were also discovered we shall not be considering their impact as the Indian Astrology believes that the nodal points, *viz.* RAHU and KETU cover their impact as well. It however, must be understood at the very outset that these heavenly bodies have not been classified in that astrophysical way. In this reckoning despite being a 'Star' the sun is also a planet and despite being a satellite the moon is also a planet. Most peculiar are the last two planets : RAHU and KETU which even don't have any physical existence as they are just the imaginary nodal points. The branch dealing with the Navagrahas' effect of these planets upon human life is called astrology. In this branch these are reckoned as live beings having their sight (Drishti or aspect) with mutually hostile and amicable relations.

It must also be understood that those who believe in the efficacy of these planet's influence also believe in astrology. Although it is supposed to be a part of the Occult sciences, for the believers in the Navagraha's influence, it is as clear as any other branch of science. The mighty sun gives us heat and light. Even a layman understands these phenomena. But the various other elements, which are directly attributable to the sun's rays can be detected only by an analysis and examination of the sun's rays by means of the spectroscope. No wonder, therefore, that the sun's rays have other properties which have not been tested by our modern scientific instruments so far— but what instrument would be more sensitive and susceptible to those influences than the human body itself ?

After all, what is this phenomenon which aggravates or abates the diseases as when the moon is full or half or a quarter ? What is the cycle that produces physical changes in woman physiologically ? What has the influence of the moon to do with the lunatics ? Why are peculiar ailments more troublesome in the morning and then increase and decrease with the heat of the sun ? If eye-sight can be effected so favourably or adversely by the heat and light of the Sun, if the pulmonary troubles can be traced to have direct and certain connections with the moon, there is no reason to disbelieve that the Sun and the moon and other heavenly bodies give out energy or substance which affect the human beings in a peculiar way. Our ignorance of the magnitude and nature of the beneficent Jupiter or the malignant Saturn, of the markedly martial Mars and luxuriously benign Venus should not shut our eyes to the overpowering influence that these planets exert over our destinies.

In fact the belief in these planets' efficacy has been a universal phenomenon right since the dawn of history. In every country and every region people have this belief that human destiny is very much dependent upon the influence of these planets. Cicero had opined centuries back that "It is fortune not wisdom that rules man's life. It is generally believed that the course of human life is pre-determined or destined by these planet's combined influence."

Of course this concept or belief has ever been a subject of controversy. There are many schools of the rationalists who refute the theory of the planetary influence making any impact upon the human life since they believe whatever a man does is the consequence of his action. But the believers in the theory of the planetary influence go a step forward to assert that even the very action is the sum total of the human effort and the planetary influence. Anyway, since this is not our topic we start with the premises that human faith in the efficacy of these nine planet's influence is beyond dispute. Even otherwise, had this not been the case these planets would not have been accorded the status of the deities. There are temples for their ritual worship and these are regularly propitiated everywhere. Since these planets determine the course of human destiny the prior knowledge of the course of life is the natural desire of every human being, ever suffering from the fear of future's unpredictability. Anything that enables one to have a peep into the future is surely most adorable. It is for this reason that despite constant adverse criticism astrology has not only stayed as the means to provide the possible peep into the future but his even been ever growing larger in its aperture.

What distinguishes these nine planets from the other deities that are worshipped is their, to some extent, visibility and their mobility. There are constantly on the move and casting their influence upon human life as they move through the twelve signs of the zodiac. Not only that the human faith in their efficacy has even minutely studied their increasing or decreasing influence in the various signs. Like human beings they have their friends and enemies among themselves and their friendship and effect get accentuated or reduced when they move in the various signs of the zodiac.

In order to assess their human like qualities given to them by the Indian School of Astrology let us have a brief discussion on their various attributes.

As we know, the twelve signs of the zodiac are the following :

ARIES, TAURUS, GEMINI, CANCER, LEO, VIRGO, LIBRA, SCORPIO, SAGITTARIUS, CAPRICORN, AQUARIUS AND PISCES.

## The Effect of the Planets in these Signs of Zodiac

The Sun : The ruler of the sign LEO, strongest in the sign ARIES and debilited in the sign LIBRA (where it is least effective).

The Moon : The ruler of the sign CANCER, strongest in the sign TAURUS and debilited or weakest in the sign SCORPIO.

Mars : Rules two signs : ARIES and SCORPIO but strongest in the sign CAPRICORN while weakest in CANCER.

Mercury : Rules two signs : GEMINI and VIRGO and strongest in VIRGO while weakest in PISCES.

Jupiter : Rules two signs : SAGITTARIUS and PISCES, exalted in CANCER and debilited or weakest in CAPRICORN.

Venus : Rules two signs : TAURUS and Libra; exalted in PISCES and debilited in VIRGO.

Saturn : Rules two signs : CAPRICORN and AQUARIUS, exalted in LIBRA and weakest in ARIES.

On the prima facie viewing these special attributes of the planets might appear illogical but once we know the basic 'human' quality or emotion represented by these planets, this classification appears not only logical but entirely convincing.

Before elaborating on that aspect we might explain that RAHU and KETU, also called the Dragon's Head and Dragon's tail respectively, are not being omitted by mistake. Many schools of the Indian Astrology deem them to be owning no sign or not getting debilited or exalted in any one of them owing to their being the shadow planets devoid of any physical existence. However, according to some schools they own or get exalted in the following signs.

RAHU is exalted in TAURUS (some opine it is GEMINI) while KETU in SCORPIO (or in SAGITTARIUS).

Since by the generally accepted principle the debilited sign of the planet is seventh from the sign the planet is exalted in, RAHU gets debilited in SCORPIO (or SAGITTARIUS) while KETU gets debilited in TAURUS or GEMINI.

## The Placement of the Planets in the Horoscope

These planets are also endowed with Drishti or aspect like the human beings, although they don't have this power uniformly distributed. While every planet is supposed to aspect the seventh sign from the sign it is posited in, Mars additionally aspects 4th and 8th signs; Jupiter, 5th and 9th rashi or signs and Saturn, 3rd and 10th signs. These signs are placed in the twelve 'houses' which are shown in the following way.

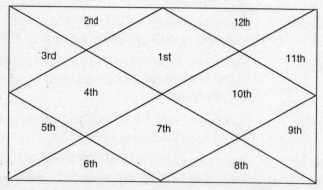

The first house is supposed to occupy the sign out of the twelve signs of zodiac which happens to be rising just above the horizon at the time of the native's birth. Native is the term used for the person whose horoscope is being considered. Suppose at that time, LIBRA is rising. Then in the first house no. 7 would be written. [It must be remembered that each of these zodiac sign is assigned a fixed number in a fixed order. So, whole ARIES is 1, TAURUS is 2, GEMINI is 3, CANCER is 4, LEO is 5, VIRGO is 6, LIBRA is 7, SCORPIO is 8, SAGITTARIUS is 9, CAPRICORN is 10, AQUARIUS is 11 and PISCES is 12].

Thus if you have the sign LIBRA or no. 7 is the first house, that chart would be the following with the ascendant Libra.

14

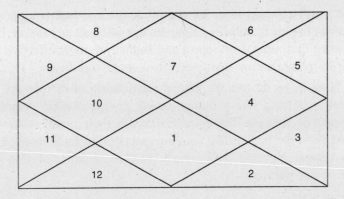

The planets are placed in the sign in accordance with their position in the particular sign at that particular moment.

Suppose we have the chart in the following way.

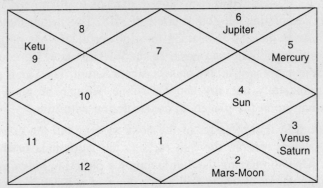

By reading the above mentioned chart we learn that the native has the Sun of Cancer sign in the 10th house; the Moon of Taurus sign in 8th house, Mars of Taurus in the 8th house; Mercury in the 11th house of Leo sign; Jupiter in the 12th house in Virgo sign; Venus in the 9th house in Gemini sign, Saturn in Gemini sign in the 9th house; Rahu of Gemini in the 9th house and Ketu of Sagittarius in the 3rd house. It must be remembered that Rahu and Ketu are always placed in the seventh house from each other. The counting of the house is done by including both the houses. Thus in the above chart the sign Aries (no. one) is seven house, apart from the Lagna or Ascendant *i.e.* the first house in which that Libra sign is placed. In the chart while Mercury aspects only 5th house. Sun only 4th house. Venus only the third house. Mars aspects 11th, 2nd and the third houses; Saturn 11th, 3rd and 6th house and Jupiter aspects 4th, 6th and 8th house. Rahu and Ketu are not assigned any aspect. It may be noted that aspects of Saturn and Jupiter are most effective while in other planet's case their position is more significant.

Now let us discuss the mutual relationship of the planets. Each planet is defined like a human being, having distinct personality, likes and dislikes etc. That is the reason why their mutual relationship, based upon the human-like emotions ascribed to each planet, appear very logical. Now we shall discuss the characteristics of each planet with in our purview[1].

## The Planets

(*i*) **The Sun.** This planet is the parent body of the solar system. The sun rules over the sign Leo and his[2] exaltation is 19 degrees of Aries. As we know that each 'house' extends to 30° to make twelve houses completing the Zodiac circle of 360°. This means that exactly at 19° Aries the Sun is deemed most powerful. He has no latitude, being always elliptic and never in the inferior state. He cooperates sympathetically with all the planets except Saturn. The Sun is deemed temperamentally hot, dry and masculine. He can be good or evil depending upon the planets in configuration with him.

The Sun is the master of the Solar system and the giver of all life. As they reckon, the Sun reckons the Atma-bala or the soul-force. A person having the Sun favourably placed in his or her chart gives the person a strong will and a sense of authority. a good Sun (preferably placed in the 10th, 11th or 3rd, 6th house) gives the person a masterful character and makes the native good administrator, traditionalist and very loyal particularly to the system. It makes the native confident and assertive. He, the sun, represents the royalty. His friends (natural allies) are Moon, Venus, Jupiter and Mercury while Mars and Saturn are supposed to be its enemies. Its favourite colour is dark red; favourite stone is Ruby and favourite metal is gold.

(*ii*) **The Moon.** The person who has strong influence of the moon has a fair stature, pale complexion, round face and phlegmatic

---

[1] That is only nine planets excluding the trans-saturnine planets.

[2] All planets are treated as masculine character in Astrology from grammatical point of view, barring Venus and Moon.

body. Moon is supposed to represent the 'Man' or the mind of the person. This native gets easily influenced by every other force since the moon is more sensitive to the influence of the signs of the Zodiac than any other planet. Moon's favourable influence upon the native makes him mild, soft, kind, ingenious and polite. The unfavourable influence is bound to make the native idle, stupid, petty and alcoholic.

The moon governs the brain, the stomach, the bowels, the bladder and according to some of the astrologers, the left eye. It also has much influence over the fluid of the body, the lymphs, glands and in case of women the breasts.

The influence of the moon makes the person quite imaginative. If the native's chart is having good aspect of Jupiter, the person becomes a learned scholar and if Venus, is well placed the person becomes a capable poet. An adverse lunar influence would make person lethargic, dirty and the day-dreamer.

When the moon is the dominant force, the native is prone to change the vocation early in life, although it might have been the stepping stone that might have led to his true work later on. It brings many fluctuations in once's career. Moon also represents the mother while the Sun the father of the native. Accordingly their good or bad influence will show its effect on the native through a devoted mother or a dotting father and a hostile mother or enmical father. Bad influence may also mark danger to the life of the native's parents.

The moon rules the populace and as such many who enjoy great popularity and who influence the masses are those that are born under the strong influence of this planet.

The moon enjoys great importance although is of negative influence because it represents sensorium. Whatever goes to man, the qualities he may posses, his ego — all these things can only come into manifestation through the medium of senses.

Being of swifter motion than the other planets, the influence of the moon is of very great importance and he forms more aspects. He indicates minor incidents, circumstances, changes and all actions of daily life. Moon in its bad position or aspect, is the most undisputed threat to the health, and can be the cause of most of the functional disorders.

The moon also governs the home. Therefore women who are natives of this planet make excellent wives and mothers. However, they are prone to love novelty, change and sensation, and as such they often find it necessary to have a large circle of acquaintances and to be given greater freedom. Without this freedom they are inclined to become restless and discontented with their domestic life. The favourite metal for the moon is silver, colour, moonshine, and gem is pearl. Fluctuating mind is the basic weakness of the native having moon as the dominant planet.

(*iii*) **Mars.** Mars is the Nayaka or Commander-in-Chief of the astral bodies in astrology. He is a planet and his nature is generally destructive. Mars is called Bhoomiputra or Bhaum-i.e. the son of the earth. He is 'Rudhira' or controller of blood and 'Rohitang' or ruddy-complexioned. It is also called Angaraka or the burning coal.

Mars is exalted in twenty eight degrees of Capricorn. He rules the signs Aries and Scorpio.

When this planet is nearest to the earth, murders are more frequent, and are of atrocious nature. When he is retrograde, innumerable calamitous and robberies take place.

A Martian native is strong, well set, but short, bony lean and muscular. He has red complexion, sharp eyes and a violent countenance. Frequently a scar is found on the head or face. A dignified or well placed Mars makes the native fearless, violent, erascible and unsubmitting. Though fond of war and contention, he is at the same time prudent, rational, over generous and magnanimous.

But an ill-placed Mars inclines the native to become violent, quarrelsome, treacherous, robber, wicked and cruel. The native has a disposition to anger, violence and possesses an eagerness to get into quarrels and mischief.

Mars governs head, face, stomach, kidneys and knees of the native's body. It is the ruler of the blood-related functions of the human body. Naturally all diseases related to blood and body heat should be ascribed to this planet. Mars is the symbol of the physical force and a lot depends on the native to utilise this force in a constructive way. It can give the native vitality, courage and ambition or at the same time make him unreasonably stubborn, intolerant, impulsive and to some extent foolhardy.

The Martian native feels only happy when he is able to conquer the enemies and overcome obstacles.

Mars's violent aspect not only causes fevers and sudden attacks of illness but also it can cause gruesome accidents, because of its quick and unexpected actions, although the aspect of a good Jupiter on Mars in the chart can help the native maintain his equilibrium and keep even temper. The native of Mars must always takes time to think out clearly his course of action and proceed from intelligently directed thought, and should not act on impulse. This native becomes an asset to the family and society if he could regulate his immense energy for constructive works. They must remember that counsel and patience are mightier than coercion.

Mars' favourite metal is copper, gem is coral and colour is blood red. In case an adverse Mars is to be propitiated, besides wearing the coral ring in the right hand middle finger, the worship of Lord Hanuman is believed to be very effective.

(iv) **Mercury.** This planet is believed to be the ruler of the mental faculties and worldwiseness; he is always close to the sun, never farther than twenty eight degrees and performs his orbit in eighty seven days and twenty three hours.

This is the most 'adjustable' planet, i.e. he immediately takes on the quality of the planets with which he is configurated and accordingly he is good, bad, lucky or unlucky. A strong Mercury makes the person tall, straight forward with deep forehead, straight nose, thin lips, narrow chin, thin narrow face, long arms, hands, fingers, thighs, legs and feet.

A good, well placed and well aspected Mercury gives its native a strong mind, active, subtle and retentive memory. It makes the native develop an eagerness in the pursuit of all kinds of knowledge. The native is a good orator, eloquent, witty and of a pleasing disposition. If, however, the native has the Mercury in conjunction with Sun, then the native is more qualified for trade than learning.

A poor Mercury makes the native possess a mean, shuffling and unprincipled character. He makes the person a liar, thief, the gambler, and a very conceited person.

People with good influence of Mercury are invariably methodical, worldwise shrewd and most adjustable in any circumstances. They know how to tackle the most ticklish situation. The ruler of this planet is said to be Vishnu.[1] Its favourite gem is emerald.

The diseases ascribed to this planet's adverse position are convulsions, stammering, apoplexy, lisping, dumbness, stoppage of humour in the nose or head, nervous cough, hoarsness, gout in the hands and feet and vertigo. An afflicted Mercury can cause mental diseases.

An exalted Mercury makes the native choose a profession connected with intellectual and literacy pursuits. The most truly sensitive of all the planets, Mercury responds to every impression. And Mercury is not modified by the signs as are the other passive planets. On the other hand, each sign excites him to give a special impression of opinion. The best influence upon Mercury is that of Saturn. Without the steadying hand of Saturn, to hold him in tutorship to a profounder wisdom, Mercury may be frivolous and vain. The native of this planet has great desire for knowledge, the longing for change and cosmopolitan spirit. They are bound to travel far and wide. They have a keen institution and ability to sense what people are about to say. A common trait of the natives of this signs is to interrupt conversations and to change the subject so quickly that others would find it difficult to follow. The native of this planet are invariably more materialistic and thus remain rather always in a hurry. That is why they are prone to suffer nervous strains. They would do well to seek association with the spiritual people and adopt somewhat altruistic approach in life. The mind of the natives of this planet is never at rest, and because of this reason they require more rest and more sleep than does the average person.

(v) **Jupiter.** Also called 'Guru', 'Jeeva' or 'Jova', it is the repository of all discretion and at the same time, the significator of money and wealth also. It is believed to be beneficial, masculine and social planet and also the author of temperance, justice and moderation. It gets exalted in five degree of cancer.

The native with Jupiterean predominance in his charts is tall, well-built, erect, handsomely proportioned, robust with a commanding personality. Such natives have oval face, high forehead, full eyes,

---

[1] Some ancient works make Ganesh as the ruler of this planet.

thick hair, wide chest, long feet and a saintly appearance. Its good influence makes the native wise, magnanimous, affable, jovial, mild in manners, temperate, just and good and naturally inclined towards religion and philosophy. Its bad influence makes the native hypocrite, indifferent, prodigal, careless, easily influenced and led astray, and a fanatic in religion. He (the native) becomes inclined to be lazy, too dependent upon luxury and too self-indulgent.

A good Jupiter also makes the native rich. His sources of income would be pure and untainted by any underhand dealing. This beneficent planet endows the native with executive ability, sound judgement and unusual vision.

Liver, veins, lungs and all the viscera is governed by Jupiter. Consequently all the diseases connected with these organs of the human body are the result of Jupiter's bad influence. Being the symbol of wisdom, Jupiter is the largest planet of the solar system. He is the dominating influence not only over man but also over everything in existence. However, his effect is modified by his exact position and aspects to the other planets. For example, if Jupiter aspects Mars, the native derives tremendous executive ability. The key word the Jupiter's influence is expansion, in contradiction to Saturn's influence being defined by contraction. Obesity of the body also falls under Jupiter's influence. Jupiter also gives instinct of creation, generosity, hospitality and of the spiritual emotions.

The favourite gem of Jupiter is 'topaz' or 'yellow-sapphire', commonly called 'Pukhraj,' and the favourite colour is bright yellow.

(*vi*) **Venus.** This is the brightest planet in the sky and is never above 45° distant from the Sun. It completes its orbit in two hundred and twenty four days and seven hours. It gets exalted precisely at 27° Pisces. Venus is the ruler of everything that is fine and sophisticated. Those natives with Venus in the dominant position in their chart are usually elegantly formed and extremely beautiful, with sparkling eyes and round or comely oval face. They have strikingly beautiful hands and feet. They usually have a wandering eye denoting desire, sweet voice and very engaging address. Venus has the effect on the native which makes the person pleasure-loving and of cultured tastes. But it makes the person choose the path of least resistance. The native will be unwilling to make sacrifices and do the hard plodding that is essential to accomplish something of great significance. These natives love poetry, music and all fine arts, wines, mild intoxicants and female company, especially of beautiful frame. An afflicted Venus makes the native profligate, indolent, shameless and open to every lust and depravity. However, as a rule the natives of this planet are mild and inoffensive.

A good Venus makes the person favourite of the king and queens, especially of the latter. He will have powerful friends who will stand by him in making his life path easy and pleasant.

Love plays a key-role in the life of the natives having dominant effect of Venus. Such natives have invariably numerous affairs and their married life is hardly happy. Venus rules jewels, perfumes, pastel shade of colours and beauty of form both in human and still life. The natives with Venus as the star of their Destiny love all best things of life including best jewels, best garments, best perfumes etc. They have a tendency to appear ostentatious. The favourite gem of Venus is diamond and the god to be worshipped for propitiating its evil effect is Lord Mahadeva (Shiv).

(*vii*) **Saturn.** The most distant among the planets under consideration (from the Sun). Saturn completes his revolution in twenty nine years one hundred sixty seven days and five hours. Which is also the duration of its one year.

Saturn is the symbol of prudence and caution. In human life, in general, the aspect of Saturn implies obstacle and delay and the exerts the force of isolation and concentration. Normally Saturn's aspect is deemed to be much more effective than its position. Saturn brings delay, and therefore makes the native despondent and hopeless.

It is believed that the influence of Saturn is most dominant during the first 30 years of a person's life, and after the sixtieth year that is during the most active years of a human beings life, although there is wide ranging dispute regarding this belief. Some of the schools claim that Saturn is effective most at and after the 36th year of the native while some scholars are of the opinion that Saturn becomes most effective even in the nativity chart when it transits the houses close to the natal sign of the native. Since this discussion is beyond the scope of the book we suspend it here but for information sake we suggest studying the Saturnian effect more when it is transisting the adverse houses.

Since Saturn is the most hurdle-causing planet all the diseases connected with any kind of blockage are represented by Saturn like acnes, epilepsy, toothache, catarrh, phthisis etc.

Those born with Saturn as their ruler of destiny must develop patience and forbearance because it always bestows even good effect in an adverse manner. Nothing is streamlined or smooth in Saturn's domain; everything is turbulent and disturbing. However, there is no denying the fact that natives with Saturn's domineering influence are known for their tenacity. They would never leave anything unfinished, no matter how daunting are the odds. They must remember that self-sacrifice and service should be the key-words of their life. No wonder most of the luminaries of the earth who burnt like meteors to en-lighten the earth had Saturn powerfully placed in their horoscopes. For them no goal is too high and no peak is unscalable. As it is believed that by forcing the native suffer all sorts of troubles and tribulations, Saturn purges then of their weakness and shortcomings and brings out the essence in them. Those with Saturn ruling their life have always gained success the harder but surer way. It always makes you happy in retrospect and never simultaneously. Comparing the influence of Saturn and Jupiter, the two biggest planets in the solar system, an analogy can be given very aptly. Jupiter's pleasure is immediate-like your having some delicious sweet whereas Saturn's pleasure in always felt in retrospect-like your taking a narcotic drug. Although immediately you would find it bitter with no tempting taste, latter on when the drugs shows it effect you feel as if you are on cloud nine.

Saturnian people are no nonsense men. They have a well defined, well thought out purpose behind their every activity. Though outwardly they might appear like 'kill-joys' and 'marplots' with no relish for fine things of life, they are the person who get full exposure of life in every way, although they invariably die in a lonely misanthropy.

Saturn's 'Sade Saati', the seven and half years duration when Saturn transits the three houses : a house preceding your moon sign, the house of the moon sign and the house following the moon sign house. Since in every sign the duration of Saturn is of two and half years, the total duration becomes of seven and half years. This cycle of Saturn's 'Sade Saati' repeats after every thirty years in a native's chart. It is not necessarily bad for everyone. However, if the first 'Sade Saati' is good then the next one is surely going to be bad. And if that person is long-aged enough to get the third 'Sade-Saati' also, that would again be good.

The favourite gem of Saturn is 'Neelam' or the blue-sapphire, favourite colour is black or dark-blue, favourite metal is iron and favourite fluid is oil. The only deity to be propitiated for quelling Saturn's adverse influence is Lord Hanuman.

(*viii*) **Rahu and Ketu.** These are in effect the Nodal points and not any physical bodies. However, these planets, called the shadowy planets, are believed to represent the sum total of the influence of the rest of the heavenly bodies felt by the earth. Although they are "shadows" and have no sight or aspect, they are considered quite influential to cast their effect upon human life. Normally, owing to their 'shadowy' nature they manifest the effect of the lord of the zodiac sign they are placed in, yet, as far as their nature is concerned, Rahu is believed to behave like 'second Saturn' and Ketu 'like second Mars'. Generally Rahu in 6th house and Ketu in 12th house are considered best, although the other aspects must also be taken into consideration.

Thus each planet has its own characteristics, potency and power innate in itself, irrespective of its position in the horoscope. The specific position in a horoscope only enhances or mitigates the basic characteristics, and indicates the trends during the life time of a person, according to the movements of the planets in the horoscope at the time of consultation.

## The Rationale Behind the Planets' Characteristic Vis-a-vis their Effect upon Human Life :

The typical human tendency is to find its reflection in every aspect of universe. When the human being detected the planets showing their influence over their life, they categorised it in conformity with their own societal norms. In human society he who is the most

24

powerful is called the king. By the same consideration they made the Sun as the king of the planets, the Moon, the queen, Mars the commander-in-chief of the forces, Jupiter the mentor or seer of their kingdom, Venus the minister for culture and other refined realms, Mercury the worldwise leader of the trader class and Saturn the leader of the masses, with Rahu its assistant while Ketu is chosen to assist Mars.

Having defined their characteristics, the human mind began to grade their effect according to the placement of the planets in the various zodiac signs ruled by a variety of planets. Now, the Sun being the owner of Leo, receives its exaltation in the sign, Aries, ruled by Mars. It is natural that the King to feel most powerful in the house of its commander-in-chief. Consequently the king has also to feel the weakest influence when placed in the sign ruled by the minister, Venus who is given to all sorts of sensual vices. Thus the Sun becomes debilited in Tula or Libra, the sign ruled by Venus. Since the Moon represents imagination it gets exaltation in Taurus, the sign ruled by Venus, again. If we take Venus to be representing all the fine arts, it is obvious that no musician or poet can excel if not supported by powerful imagination ? And in the house of Mars, that is in Scorpio the moon becomes weakest for the obvious reason that imagination has no scope in the army of physical forces where the watch-word is discipline. How can imagination excel in a section ruled by discipline ? Then comes, Mars, the commander-in-chief. The arena to show his maximum valour for the C in C is the house of its sworn enemy i.e. Saturn. So Mars gets exaltation in Capricorn, the house ruled by Saturn. And for the same reason which makes the moon weakest in the house of Mars, Mars also gets debilited in the house of moon, i.e. in Cancer or Karka. Owing to Mercury being the most worldwise and adjustable planet, it can adjust itself well in every condition. So it is the only planet which gets exaltation in Virgo, its own sign. If Jupiter represents discretionary knowledge what good can the knowledge do without the support of imagination ? Hence Jupiter gets exalted in Karka or Cancer, the sign ruled by Moon. And we also know that, generally, the high level of knowledge to masses is of no use to them because the lack indiscretion is likely to make them put that to misuse. That is why Jupiter gets debilited in Capricorn, the sign ruled by Saturn. Venus being the ruler of all that is fine gets exaltation in Pisces because the repertoire of the fine arts gets its due recognition only when supported by the discretionary wisdom, that is by the powerful Jupiter. Hence Venus' exaltation in Pisces. This planet, Venus gets debilited in the sign of Mercury, that is Virgo. Why ? Because this ostentatious planet, given to sensual enjoyment has no place in the house governed by the most worldwise planet, Mercury. Would a Wajid Ali Shah care for money when holding his 'Raas' performances or the famous "Inder-sabhaas". Hence the Virgo is the debilitation sign for Venus. Now, Saturn represents all that is crude and base, desiderating for refinement. Hence the exaltation sign for Saturn is Tula or Libra the sign ruled by the ruler of refinement Venus. And lastly, how can a leader of the masses excel in the house ruled by Mars the agent implementing all that is held precious by tradition. Hence Saturn gets debilited in Aries, the sign ruled by Mars, the commander-in-chief which allows the king, the Sun, to blossom to his full majesty in this sign.

As a matter of fact, once you have known the basic characters of the planet, you might automatically realise why it is debilited in a particular sign and exalted in the given sign only. In general, the exaltation sign of the planet is 180° apart from the sign of its debilitation. These planets also rule over certain groups of stars called the constellation. It is from the placement of the planets, particularly the Moon, that the Dasha, Antardasha or Pratyantra[1] Dasha are calculated. The planets with the duration of their major period alongwith their rulership of the constellation are shown below in the chart.

| Sun Dasha | Moon | Mars | Rahu | Jupiter | Saturn | Merc. | Ketu | Venus |
|---|---|---|---|---|---|---|---|---|
| 6 yrs | 10 yrs | 7 yrs | 18 yrs | 16 yrs | 19 yrs | 17 yrs | 7 yrs | 20 yrs |
| Krittika | Rohini | Mriga-shira | Aadra | Punar-vasu | Pushya | Ashlesha | Magha | Poorva-Falguni |
| Uttra Falguni | Hasta | Chitra | Swati | Vishaa-kha | Anura-dha | Jyeshtha | Moola | Bharani |
| Uttra-ashaa-dha | Shrawan | Dhani-shtha | Shata-bhisha | Poorva-bhandra-pad | Uttra-bhadra-pad | Revati | Ashwani | Poorva ashaa-dha |

1. Main, minor, sub-minor periods respectively. See a full chapter ahead on the Dasha system.

There are 27 constellations or asterisms which have definite influence on the physical and mental characteristics of the person. The asterism in which the Moon is placed at the time of birth is of a great significance. The Janma-Nakshatra shows the position of the moon in the asterism at the time of birth.

The longitudinal degrees of the asterism are given below alongwith their English equivalent.

| Nakshatra | Asterism | Longitude |
|---|---|---|
| Ashwini | Beta Arietis | 13°20′ |
| Bharani | 35 Arietis | 26°20′ |
| Kritika | Eta Tauri | 40° |
| Rohini | Aldebaran | 53°20′ |
| Mrigshira | Lambada Orionis | 66°40′ |
| Ardra | Alpha Orionis | 80°0′ |
| Punarvasu | Beta Geminiorium | 92°20′ |
| Pushya | Delta Cancri | 106°40′ |
| Ashlesha | Alpha Hudroe | 120°0′ |
| Makha | Regulus | 133°20′ |
| Poorva Phalguni | Delta Leonis | 146°40′ |
| Uttava Phalguni | Beta Leovis | 160°0′ |
| Hasta | Delta Corvi | 173°20′ |
| Chitra | Spicia Virgins | 186°40′ |
| Swati | Arcturus | 200°0′ |
| Vishakha | Alpha Libroe | 213°20′ |
| Anuradha | Delta Scorpio | 226°40′ |
| Jyeshtha | Avtares | 240°0′ |
| Moola | Lambada Scorpii | 253°0′ |
| Poorva Ashadha | Delta Sagitlani | 266°40′ |
| Uttara-Ashadha | Sigma Sagittari | 280°0′ |
| Shravana | Alpha Aquiloe | 293°20′ |
| Dhanishtha | Beta Delphinum | 306°40′ |
| Shata-Bhisha | Lambda Aquarius | 320°0′ |
| Poorva Bharapada | Alpha pafasi | 333°0′ |
| Uttra Bhadrapada | Gama Pegasi | 346°40′ |
| Revati | Zeta Piscum | 360°0′ |

It may be seen that each asterism's duration is 13°20' and since each sign is of 30°. When the planet travels in each sign, it covers little more than two nakshatras or the constellation in each sign. When the moon is passing through a 'Pada' (or part of the asterism each extending to 3°20') of some particular asterism at birth, the effects can be very harmful to the child, mother or the father. If, however, the evil effects are averted owing to other benevolent planetary combinations the child may live upto ripe old age, and enjoy great prosperity and glory in life. In particular 1st pada of Moola, 4th pada of Ashlesha, 1st pada of Makha or 4th pada of Jyeshtha can be very dangerous for the child getting birth in it.

Since all these asterism have a distinct planet's rulership as mentioned earlier, each of them has a definite influence upon the child. For example the natives of Rohini usually have exceptionally large eyes. They are generally honest and truthful in their dealings and generous. Charitable to a fault. they are good conversationalist; they have very keen and steadfast wisdom. For more details the reader is advised to consult some standard work on Indian astrology.

## House Division

These nine planets are ever on move. But they cast two types of effect upon the native. One is called transit influence and the other is called the nativity's or the natal chart influence. It is because the natal chart is supposed to be the exact position of the planet right at the time of the native's birth. But after the birth, the planets don't cease to move; they keep on moving, casting a comparatively milder effect upon the native. Before 32 years of age the percentage of effect of the two types of influences is 60%, 40% which gets reversed after 32nd year.

As we have already discussed, the first house of the chart is called the ascendant which is studied to learn about the native's basic personality and face related problems. The second house is the house of reserves, voice, and all the human organs upto throat. The third house covers brothers, arms and valour of the person. The fourth house is of mother, heart, vehicles, pleasure, home and landed property. The fifth house represents, life after death, and procreation, that is : your mental faculties and your progeny and the body organs between heart and liver. The sixth house covers maternal uncle, diseases and enemies. The seventh rules your dealing with the other party, including your wife/husband, business partners etc. The pleasures of bed and affairs are judged together with the 5th and 7th house. The 8th house is the house of anus region and death and everything related with the dead objects including land. The 9th house represents your religious faith, luck, ancestors, thighs and life before birth. The 10th house is the house of action, father and the knee region. The 11th house is the house of income from every source, elderly relations, and the shin region. The 12th house is the house of dissipation, salvation and philanthropy and relates to feet region of the body.

Thus when the planets are placed in these houses in given signs under the relevant constellation their effect upon the native's life is determined by studying the following variables. Then your prediction is the locus of these variables, as they call in mathematical jargon.

(a) Planet's position in the house.

(b) Planet's position in the sign.

(c) The Moon's position in the asterism.

(d) The other planet's mutual aspect.

(e) The planet's rulership of the asterisms.

All these factors help you study the horoscope and make your prediction. But as the famous shloka asserts :

"Phalani grahacharena soochiyanti maneeshinah |
Ko vakta taartamyasya tamekam vedhasam vina ||"

[The learned scholars indicate in a way what will take place in future (But) who else, except the Creator Brahma can say with certainly what will definitely happen ?]

It is only this doubt that makes astrology only an occult science. All these planets do indicate the course of destiny but not with any certainty. The exact science on the other hand is able to tell you the exact relationship between the cause and effect. Nevertheless, the planetary influence has come to be studied by man for many millennia so there is no denying the fact that these planets do cast their effect upon human life.

It is the effect of the planets particularly in life and over all the animate and inanimate world in general that has accorded these planets a status not less than that of a deity. There are many temples of the Navagraha in India. It is not an uncommon site to see even the most western looking Indian secretly dropping the coins in an oil filled jar with a bizarre figure-believed to be of Saturn-only for the sake of propitiating this most fastidious planet. The worship of the Sun and the moon, must have started not for their only being the natural source of light but their casting their definite effect on the course of human destiny.

Giving this brief knowledge of astrology was deemed necessary for realising the basic effect of the planets upon human system. In the following pages we shall be discussing the planets' astronomical, mythological and cultural significance, mutual relationships and ethos. Many of the astronomical relationships have been turned into mythological allegories only for bringing home the point by the ancient seers and scholars. As has been the wont of the ancient Indians they never saw life in different pieces but as an integrated whole unit. That is why we find many astrological belief showing their manifestations in different spheres of life. In fact many astrological words have entered into our lingua franca so deeply that it is difficult to find a matching expression in modern parlance. For example, it is very common to chide a person becoming too choosy or finicky by saying : "Meena and Makha mat nikalo" in Hindi. It simply means the person is trying to be extra cautions in calculations and determining a fact. Needless to remind our leaders that Mesh is Aries and Meen is Pisces in Sanskrit. Similarly an adverse relationship between two individuals is also defined as 6th and 8th relationship. It is so because in astrology the 6th, 8th relationship between two planets is bad whereas 5th and 9th relationship is deemed very good.

## The Navamsha Chart

The Lagna chart (showing the Lagna and various planets' position) and the moon chart (making the moon sign placed in the first house and the rest of the planets in the signs as in the Lagna chart) have already been hinted at. While studying the horoscope both of these charts must be scrutinised. It is the belief of the celebrated astrologers that both of these charts cast their impact on the final happening in a native's life. But they believe they act in 60 : 40 ratio. That is, till 32 years of age the Lagna chart gets 60 percent importance in the prediction while the moon chart only 40 percent but after 32 their significance gets reversed. That is, the moon chart gets 60 percent importance and the Lagna (Ascendant) chart 40 percent. The argument is that after thirty two it is the mind which is called most into play for taking decision than body. Since the moon chart represents the native's mental make-up it gets more importance than the Lagna chart which chiefly reveals one's physical capabilities. Hence the variation in the importance of the two charts at advanced age.

There is, however, yet another chart which must be studied chiefly for ascertaining the inherent strength of the planets. That is called the Navamsha chart. In fact the Lagna chart reveals only a sketch of the positions of the planets, and to get greater precision of the positions of the cusps and planets there is a system of more accurate form of recording these positions in the Indian astrology. This is done by getting the Navamsha chart. Normally when you get your chart made by some professional agency, this chart is also given alongside. In this chart every sign is divided into 9 equal parts and each part has a rulership of a particular planet who rules over the complete sign in the natural order (viz Aries, Taurus etc.). For example Aries (Mesha) is divided in to equal parts; We know that each rashi or house has 30°. So divided by 9 in Mesha the first part, that is. upto 3°20′ [30°÷ 9 = 3°20′]. Which is ruled by the ruler of Mesha-Mars. And the second part, that is upto 6°40′ is ruled by the ruler of Taurus or Vishakha. which is Venus, so on and so forth. Therefore in order to place a particular planet in a particular house we have to find in which of the 108 divisions each longitude falls, and following that order, we have to place the planet or cusp of the ascendant in different signs. The following is the Navamsha chart of the Lagna chart given before :

For all practical purposes, what one should study from the Navamsha chart is the strength of a planet. Suppose one has an exalted Jupiter in the Lagna Chart but Jupiter occupies the debilited sign-Capricorn in the Navamsha Chart. In that case the intransic strength of Jupiter gets reduced to only 50 percent. Hence it won't be as efficacious as it might have been had Jupiter been in a powerful sign or in his own sign. Also, if a planet gets the same sign in the

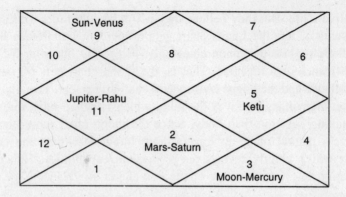

Navamsha chart as it is in the Lagna or moon chart,[1] the planet is said to be of Vargottam category which means that the planet is as strong as it would be on occupying his own sign. In the chart given below, Mars enjoys this positions since it is in Taurus [Vrishabha or the sign no 2] in the native chart as well as in the Navamsha Chart. Hence it should be deemed as powerful as if it is either in Mesha or Scorpio—that is in its own signs.

Navamsha Chart plays a very important role in the evaluation of a horoscope, as can to seen from the above statement.

## General Guidelines

While ascertaining the strength of the Bhavas (the houses) in a horoscope, the important considerations are as follows :

(*i*) Assuming that the lord of the Bhava is strong by his position— for example he is tenating a friend's house whether he is so in the Lagna Kundali or the Navamsha Kundali (Chart).

(*ii*) Whether the friend, whose house he is tenating happens to be weak or strong. If he is weak, then the original Bhava also becomes very weak.

(*iii*) If the dispositors [the owner of the sign the planets are placed in] are strong by exalted positions or in friends or own place, then the original Bhavas though weak by themselves, become strong.

---

[1] Moon Chart is made by placing the Lagna Chart's moon sign in the 1st house and the rest of the planets in the sign as shown in the lagna-chart.

A Bhava is considered to be strong, when friends of its lord, his exalted lord, the planet to which that Bhava is exalted occupy 11th, 2nd or 3rd positions. However, if these planets are weak, combust or the enemies to the houses, the opposite will be the result. Here again we must bear in mind the following three points :

(a) The strength of a Bhava is proportionate to its Navamsha.

(b) Malefic influences, predominating on the Bhavas will destroy them.

(c) If the lord of the Lagna has a good aspect to a particular Bhava, this will mean auspicious results. But then if a malefic planet happens to be the lord of the Bhava and aspects the same, the result will be the opposite.

Moreover, the nature of a house indication can be predicted only from the nature of the influence that house receives. Suppose we are evaluating the seventh house, an aspect to this house from the lord of the 6th house will mean trouble in marriage through enemies; aspect of the lord of the 12th house means poverty or dissipation of the resources and an aspect of the lord of the 8th house will mean danger to life from matrimonial relations.

Remember that opposite indication of two different planets do not mean that they destroy each other. Each will have its own individual effect.

However, when a planet has the rulership of two houses, there is an unusual situation of the planet bestowing to conflicting effects on a single bhava. In such a case the stronger of the two will prevail.

To decide the question of direction with reference to a Bhava, one of these points have to be taken into consideration.

(i) The planet aspecting it

(ii) Lord of the Bhava

(iii) Planet tenating it

(iv) The Navamsha of the lord of the Bhava

(v) The Navamsha of the Bhava Karaka.[1]

---

[1] Karaka means significator of a house, like Mars is of the 6th house, Sun of the 10th and so on. It means that they are more effective in these houses.

A Bhava becomes effective when the lord of the Lagna or the lord of the Bhava, the Karaka planet or Jupiter transits the Bhava or the houses occupied by the lord of the Bhava either in the Rashi Kundali or in the Navamsha Kundali (Chart). And when the eighth house lord transits any of the above houses the Bhava may be considered defective.

Now we shall be confining our study to planetary effects on health of an individual, that is, the main topic of the book.

---

[1] Transit effects are given ahead.

# CHAPTER THREE

# Planets and the Parts of the Body

According to the ancient treaties on astrology each planet has a definite influence on various parts, functions etc. of the human body. They have been summed up in the following manner

**Sun** : Heart, circulatory system, right eye, spleen, blood, stomach, bones, head, thyroid, brain, pituitary, bilious complaints, skin, boils, eruptions.

**Moon** : Digestive and bronchial systems, tumours, inherited disorders, jaundice, epilepsy, cold, nausea, mental disorders, uterus, breast, lungs, blood, diarrhoea, alimentary canal, phlegons and white corpuscular disorders.

**Mars** : Accidents, blood, inflammatory ailments, genitals (male), piles, arteries, veins, nose, neck, rectum, marrow, gonad, adrenaline, muscles, red corpuscles, bile, fever, spleen, boils, small pox, blood pressure.

**Mercury** : Respiratory system, asthma, speech, nervous system, chest, skin, navel, nose, gall-bladder, pancreas, parathyroid, brain, epilepsy (induced one) neurastherin, muscular tissues; itches, falls, shivering.

**Jupiter** : Congestion, liver, arteries, hips, thighs, tongue, ear, brain, spleen, pancreas, gout, abnormal growth, diabetes, fainting, swelling in legs, pain on the right side.

**Venus** : Liver Kidney, eye-sight, face, glands, ovaries, hair, neck, leucoder, consumption, ulcer, diphtheria, thyroid, semen, urine, throat, veins.

| Saturn | : | Skin, bones, knees, feet, gall bladder, teeth, leg, arthritis, adrenalin, ligaments, toxins, minerals, salts, rheumatism. |
|---|---|---|
| Rahu | : | Feet, breathing, spine, leprosy, pains in the joints. |
| Ketu | : | Belly; disorders due to fear or affliction of evil spirits. |

In general chronic disease refer to Saturn, acute ones involve Mars and Rahu.

Now we will take up some specific ailments and their relations with the planets.

**Appendicitis** : Afflicted moon and the 6th house are to be noted. Mars with Ketu can also afflict this part. Hair involves Mars, Mercury and Saturn. Right hand relates to Rahu and the third house which Mars relates to left hand; also consider 11th house. Waist is governed by Rahu while Saturn also casts its impact on spleen. Venus relates to right thigh while Saturn rules over right foot. Sun relates to left foot. Jupiter and Ketu cast their specific influence on intestines but Jupiter and Rahu combination exerts greater over stomach region.

**Head** : Afflicted Sun and Mars. Brain-Sun and Mercury. Neck-Mars, Rahu and the third house. Bones-Sun, Mars, Saturn and Rahu. Arthritis-Saturn and houses 1, 6, 8, 12. Heart-4th and 5th house, Sun, Mars and Mercury in the 4th or 5th. Lungs and Chest-Moon and the 4th house. Kidney-Venus, Libra and the 7th house. Liver-Sun, Jupiter; 5th house and Leo.

**Ear** : Gemini and Virgo, Mercury; Mars & Rahu in 3rd; lord of 2nd in 1st or 8th. The Right ear afflictions refer to Jupiter and the 3rd house. Left ear refers to Mars and the 11th house. Tongue-Rahu, Saturn and the houses 6, 8, 12.

**Eye** : Sun, Venus, houses 2 and 12 should be considered. Also Moon, Mars, Saturn and Rahu are to be examined. Right eye involves the Sun and the 2nd house. Left eye refers to the Moon and the 12th house.

**Nose** : Saturn and the Moon, houses 6, 8, 12.

**Teeth** : Rahu and Saturn in 2nd ; associated with the lord of Lagna. Mercury and Saturn should also be considered.

**Skin** : Saturn is the chief indicator alongwith Mars; houses 1, 6, 8 are to be considered Leucoderma refer to Venus.

**Diabetes** : Jupiter, Venus and the Sun.

**Generative Organs** : Mars, Venus and Rahu, houses 7th, 8th, 9th and 12th are to be examined urinary disorders refer to the Moon and Mars.

**Hydrocele** : Mars, Saturn, Rahu in lagna (ascendant) lord of 1st in 8th with Rahu; and Jupiter and Rahu in Lagna.

**Leprosy** : There are many combinations chiefly involving houses 1 and 6. The huminaries (the Sun and the Moon), Mars, Saturn, Mercury and the Nodes (Rahu & Ketu) should also be considered. Prime indicators are Mars and Rahu.

**Tuberculosis (T.B.)** : Consider houses 1, 6 and 8th. Mercury with Mars in 6th aspected by the Moon and Venus. Saturn is the chief indicator. Mars and Nodes (Rahu and Ketu) are to be considered. Aspect of the Moon is also significant.

**Paralysis** : Saturn with Jupiter in Gemini Libra or Aquarius in the 6th; the Moon and Mercury afflicted by Saturn and Rahu; the Sun in Lagna affected by Mars and Saturn in Leo or in houses owned by Mars.

**Mental Afflictions** : Of the mental afflictions, insanity is the dominant one. The house involved are 3rd, 5th, and 9th; at times consider 7th also. The relevant combinations includes Jupiter in the 1st, Mars is the 7th; Saturn in the 1st and Mars in the 5th; 7th and 9th. The Moon, Mars and Mercury in one Kendra; conjunction of the Moon, Saturn and Ketu; Mars and Mercury in the 6th or 8th.

# Planetary Effect on Glands :

The planets governing the glands are the following :

(*a*) Sun : Thyroid, front pituitary

(*b*) Moon : Thyroid

(*c*) Moon and Mars : Beck pituitary

(*d*) Mars and Ketu : Pineal

(*e*) Mars and Saturn : Parathyroid

(*f*) Mars and Jupiter : Thyroid

(*g*) Mars, Jupiter and Venus : Pancreas

(*h*) Mars and Venus : Adrenalin and sex glands

(i) Mars : Adrenalin, gonad

(j) Mercury : Back Pituitary, Parathyroid

(k) Venus : Pancreas

(l) Saturn : Pituitary, adrenalin

(m) Rahu and Ketu : Parathyroid and Pineal.

Many physical ailments have a reference to the part played by Mars, Saturn and Rahu. Rahu and Ketu's effect refers to poisoning. As is apparent there is lot of overlapping in the planet's hold upon the various body organs and parts. This is due to the reason that human body can not be divided into water-tight compartments. An organ's affliction could be caused by various external and internal factors. A disorder in the head could very well have its origin in some glandular malfunctioning.

These should be treated as general guide lines. Now we shall be discussing the native's susceptibility to particular ailments vis-a-vis the particular ascendant or lagna.

# CHAPTER FOUR

# Ascendant-wise Disease Proveness

## A. Aries Ascendant

1. In Aries ascendant if Mercury be lord of 6th house and afflicted by bad planets' aspect, the native gets blind by getting hurt from a fast water current.

2. If the lord of the 4th the Moon be hemmed among the malefics in this ascendant (Aries), the native is prone to getting afflicted with a heart disease.

3. If the 4th lord Moon, be weak and placed in Gemini, Virgo or Scorpio : heart ailment.

4. If Moon be in 8th house with Mars : heart ailment.

5. If Saturn be in Cancer, lord of the 6th Mercury and Sun placed with malefics : heart ailment is the result.

6. 'Jataka Panjak' claims that if 4 or 5th house be occupied by malefics, heart ailment is the likely consequence.

7. If Rahu be in the fourth house aspected by malefics and the lord of the lagna (ascendant) be weak the native is prone to suffer heart attack.

8. If the Sun be in Scorpio hemmed in or aspected by malefics, heart attack is the most likely consequence.

9. Mars + Moon + Saturn be placed to a bad house : possibility of death in a vehicle accident.

10. If Mars and Saturn be in the lagna (1st house), Moon in the 4th, Sun and Jupiter be in 12th, in the middle age the native gets afflicted with severe Jaundice or any ailment caused by bile and blood's unhealthy mixture.

11. If a malefic or malefics be in the ascendant (1st house) with the ruler of the lagna (Mars) powerless, the native becomes a chronic patient.

12. The Moon weak in digital strength be placed in the ascendant and receiving aspect from malefics : Chronic illness to the native.

13. Mars in 4th, Mercury and Saturn in 12th : the native is likely to be afflicted with leprosy.

14. Leprosy is possible if Moon and Saturn be in the ascendant and Jupiter be in the 6th house.

15. Exalted Jupiter in a Kendra house (1, 4, 7, 10) Mercury in 5th or 9th and the ascendant lord Mars be powerful, the native attains full age (80 yrs.)

16. If the ascendant lord (Mars) be aspecting 1st house with all benefics in the kendra houses the native lives upto 75 years.

17. Mars in 5th of Leo and the Sun of Libra in 7th make the native live upto 70 years in good health.

18. Saturn in 1st, Moon of Cancer in 4th, Mars in 7th and the Sun in 10th with any benefic — this combination makes the native live like a king and pass away around 60 years.

19. Lord of the 8th, Mars be in 7th, Moon in 6th or 8th with malefics — this combination lets the native live upto only 55 years.

20. Saturn in 1st with any planet, Moon in 8th or 12th make the native a man of principles and erudition but he or she may live upto only 52 years.

21. Powerful Moon in the lagna and 120° apart from the sun : the native enjoys all kingly comforts but passes away at 48 years age only.

22. In the Moon be in Virgo or Scorpio of this movable sign[1] lagna (Aries) and not aspected by benefics with no benefic in any Kendra (1, 4, 7, 10) the native lives only upto 33 years.

---

[1] All the signs are categorised in three sections : Movable, stable and dual signs. Starting from the sign Aries this order is movable, stable and dual. Thus the signs are : Aries-movable; Taurus-stable, Gemini-duel; Cancer-movable, Leo-dual Virgo-stable and so on.

23. If Mars and Saturn be placed in this lagna with Jupiter in 6th or Moon in 8th, the native lives for 32 years.

24. An evil planet in 2nd or 12th, lord of lagna he weak and the 2nd or 12th not aspected by benefics—the native lives for 32 years only.

25. Jupiter in the lagna (Aries), Mars in Pisces cause early death combination with the possibility of the native not living beyond 12 years.

26. In this lagna if the Sun be in 7th with Rahu the native suffers early death of his or her mother.

27. Saturn in 1st house (in Aries) with Rahu or Ketu also causes early death of his or her mother.

28. If the 1st house or its lord be hemmed between malefics, malefic be in 7th and the lord of soul, the Sun be weak, the native may commit suicide in utter desperation.

29. If weak Moon be together with Saturn in 8th such native falls victim to evil spirits influence and dies very early.

## B. Taurus Ascendant

1. Lord of the 6th, Venus be in 1st aspected by malefics the native becomes blind due to a water-borne disease.

2. Heart ailment is the consequence if in this ascendant 4th house be occupied by a malefic or the 4th lord Sun be hemmed between the evil planet.

3. Presence of Saturn in 4th (of Leo) and lord of 6th Venus be aspected by evil planets make the native suffer heart diseases.

4. Lord of ascendant Venus be weak with Rahu in 4th makes the native suffer heart ailment.

5. If Venus, Sun and Guru (Jupiter) he posited together in 6th, 8th, or 12th house, the possibility of the native getting killed in accident cannot be ruled out.

6. If a weak Moon be placed in this Taurus Lagna with the 1st house aspected by a malefic, the native remains a chronic patient.

7. If Venus be in 4th or 12th house with Mars and Mercury the native may become victim of leprosy. The same is the result if Saturn and Moon be placed in 6th house with Jupiter.

41

8. Saturn of Aries in 12th, Mars in 5th of Virgo and Sun in 7th of Scorpio make the native survive for full age i.e. 72 years.

9. The native is an erudite scholar if in Taurus ascendant Jupiter be placed in the Kendra houses even with the malefics. But such a native is not likely to be long aged and may cross barely 60 years.

10. If lord of 7th be in 8th—particularly Jupiter and the Moon be placed with the malefics, the native may two upto 58 years.

11. If the lord of the lagna Venus be placed with malefics, lord of 8th Jupiter be in 6th with malefics with no benefics aspecting either of the planets, the native may not have long life.

12. Moon in 8th, Jupiter in 6th and Saturn + Mars be in the lagna the native may not cross 36 years in life.

13. The sun in 6th alongwith Rahu or Ketu may cause untimely death to his or her mother.

14. If the lagna lord Venus be hemmed between two malefies with 7th also occupied by an adverse malefic and the Sun itself be weak, the native might commit suicide in utter desperation.

15. The native suffers from some divine curse if Moon be placed among the malefics and Saturn be placed in 7th.

16. Evil spirits disturb the native if a week Moon be placed in 8th with Saturn.

## C. Gemini Ascendant

1. If the lord of the 6th house, Mars be placed in the lagna with malefics aspecting it, the native is likely to fall victim to dropsy.

2. If the 4th lord Mercury be placed in the company of evil planets, the native is likely to suffer heart trouble.

3. If 4th lord Mercury be placed with 8th lord Saturn in 8th itself the native is likely to suffer cardiac problems.

4. If the lord of 4th Mercury be placed in Cancer or Pisces or be combust the native feels a shooting pain in the heart region.

5. If Saturn be in 4th house (in Virgo), 6th lord Mars and Sun be placed among the evil planets or benefics the native is likely to suffer infarction of heart.

6. If Rahu in 4th be receiving evil aspect from other malefic and the lagna lord Mercury be weak the native suffers from a shooting pain in the heart region.

7. If there be conjunction of Mercury, Saturn and Mars in bad houses particularly in 6th, 8th and 12th the native may die in an accident.

8. An evil plant in the lagna with lord of lagna, Mercury, be weak the native remains perpetually ill.

9. Rahu in 4th house, Moon in 6th unaspected by benefic makes the native die even in his childhood.

10. The conjunction of Sun, Rahu, Jupiter and Mars in 8th house for this lagna and the placement of Venus—unaspected by benefics in 8th — make the life very hard and full of a variety of ailments for the native.

11. The lagna lord Mercury, if hammed between the malefics with no auspicious planet casting its aspect on it, and the Sun be weak make the native commit suicide.

12. A weak Moon with Saturn in 8th makes the native fall victim be the troubles caused by the evil spirits.

# D. Cancer Ascendant

1. The Sun, 7th from the lagna, makes the native face recurrent eye-troubles.

2. Evil planets in 4th and the 4th lord Venus hemmed between malefics make the native susceptible to heart troubles.

3. If the 4th lord Venus be in Virgo or Leo sign or be combust, the native may face heart troubles.

4. Saturn in Libra in 4th, Sun in Aquarius in 8th also cause heart troubles.

5. If Sun in Scorpio be hemmed between two evil planets the native may face a shooting pair in the heart region.

6. Moon, Venus and Saturn be together in a bad house (6th, 8th or 12th) with Mars aspecting them may make the native die in a accident.

7. If the Moon be in 1st or Scorpio (5th house) or Pisces (9th) the native remains mostly healthy and robust.

8. Jupiter in the lagna (1st house), Mars in Capricorn, Venus in Pisces or Taurus and all other planets be in Kendra houses (1, 4, 7, 10) : the native lives for a complete human life span i.e. 120 years.

9. Moon and Saturn together in 7th, unaspected by benefics or evil planets make the native live for more than 100 years.

10. If the lord of 8th Saturn be placed in 5th or 9th and aspected by strong Jupiter or Venus make the native live for 100 years.

11. Moon be in the 6th house (of Sagittarius), no evil planet or malefic in 8th and all the auspicious planets (Jupiter or Venus) in Kendra make the native live for 86 years.

12. Jupiter + Mercury + Sun in 1st(Cancer), Saturn in Pisces and the Moon in 12th form a kind of 'Rajayoga'. Such natives live like a king but live only for 66 years.

13. Saturn in Lagna, Moon in 4th, exalted Mars in 7th, exalted Sun in 10th with a benefic make the native lead a royal life but die at 60 years of age.

14. Mars and Saturn be together in the lagna, Moon be in 8th : the native becomes an erudite scholar but such natives do not live long and pass away at 52 years of age.

15. Saturn and Mars in lagna, Moon in 8th and Jupiter in 6th unaspected by benefics : the native dies at 32 years of age.

16. Saturn hemmed between two malefics (count Rahu and Ketu also among the malefics), Moon receiving aspect from an evil planet and be weak in digital strength : the native gets killed by a weapon blow dealt by his own assistant around 67 years.

17. Sun + Mars be in 8th, the lord of the lagna Moon be weak with no auspicious aspect : the nature dies early in adolescent age.

18. Sun in 4th, Jupiter in 8th, Moon in 12th unaspected by benefics : the child won't survive after its birth and may die in a month's time.

19. Saturn in 10th with Rahu or Ketu : the child may survive but his mother would die soon.

20. 6th lord Jupiter in 7th or 10th; Mars aspecting 1st house : the native may suffer some divine affliction.

21. If the lord of the lagna, Moon and the lagna (1st house) itself be hemmed between malefics with an evil planet be in 7th, the native may commit suicide.

## E. Leo Ascendant

1. Sun in the 7th causes eye-trouble for the native of this ascendant.

2. Saturn in the lagna may cause blindness. The native of this lagna with Saturn in 1st may also make the native squint-eyed.

3. If either Sun or Moon be placed in 1st and aspected by Mars or Saturn : the native may lose his vision.

4. If the 4th lord Mars be placed with the 8th lord Jupiter in 8th house : the native may suffer heart ailments.

5. If malefics be placed in 4th or 5th house the native of this lagna may suffer heart ailment.

6. If the lord of the lagna (Sun) be hemmed between two malefics in Scorpio, the native may suffer heart attack.

7. Moon in Capricorn, no evil planet in 8th and benefic planets placed in Kendra houses; the native may live well beyond 80.

8. If Mercury—Venus Combination be placed in Kendra (1, 4, 7, 10) or trikona (5, 9) houses and Mars be in 10th house of Scorpio, the native may live for full age (beyond 80).

9. Saturn in the lagna (ascendant or 1st house) Moon of Scorpio in 4th, Mars in 7th and Sun in 10th with Jupiter or Venus the native may enjoy a royal life but die around 60 years of age.

10. Saturn + Mars in lagna, Moon in 8th, Jupiter in 6th : the native may die at 32 years of age (if there be no redeeming aspect)

11. If there be an exchange of the house ownership between Jupiter in Aries and Mars in Pisces the native may die well with in teens.

12. If unaspected by any benefic planet the combination of Rahu + Venus + Sun be present in 2nd house in Virgo sign, such a native may cause death of his father and soon may kill himself as well.

13. Lord of the lagna (1st house), Sun, and the house itself be hemmed between malefics, 7th be occupied with Saturn and weak Moon : the native may commit suicide.

14. Weak Moon be in 1st with some evil planet (count Rahu & Ketu also among them) the native may die due to torture inflicted by his enemy.

15. Mars with Rahu or Ketu be in 12th house : the native's mother may die during child bearing stage.

16. A sickly life is indicated if Jupiter + Rahu + Sun + Mars be in 7th and Venus be in 7th (of Aquarius).

17. Sun in lagna but hemmed between two malefics, (being placed in 2nd or 12th) with 1st house receiving evil aspect from an adversely placed Mars : the native may die in an explosion or may be killed by a weapon during a fight in its 47th year.

# F. Virgo Ascendant

1. If the lord of 4th, Jupiter, be hemmed between malefic with a malefic be placed in 4th, the native may suffer heart ailment.

2. If the 4th lord Jupiter be in 8th together with eighth lord Mars : the native is prone to getting heart attacks.

3. If the 4th lord Jupiter be in its debilited sign Capricorn or be combust due to its proximity to Sun, heart ailment is the consequence.

4. Placement of evil planets in 4th or 5th house also make the native suffer heart ailment.

5. Sun in Scorpio hemmed between malefics makes the native suffer shooting pain in the heart region.

6. If Mercury, Jupiter and Mars' combination be in a bad house (6th, 8th, 12th) the native may die in an accident.

7. If the 1st house be occupied by an evil planet or aspected by it or a weak moon be placed in it, the native may remain perpetually ill.

8. If the lord of the ascendant, Mercury be placed in the 4th house alongwith Mars or Saturn, the native may become a leper. The same is the result if this combination be in 12th house.

9. If Venus and Saturn be in 1st house and Jupiter be aspected by Mars, the native may have problem with his semen.

10. Saturn for this legna's native be placed in 2nd with Rahu in 12th, the native may become diabetic.

11. Saturn, debilited, be placed in 8th (in Aries) the native suffers from urinary problems.

12. For Virgo ascendant if Mars and Venus be in 6th, aspected by Saturn or Jupiter : the native becomes patient of ulcerative colitis.

13. Moon in 8th, Mercury + Sun + Mars be in any house, blood pressure problem is likely to prove fatal for the native.

14. For Virgo ascendant, Saturn and Sun be in 7th, Mercury and Moon be in 6th : the native becomes patient of epilepsy.

15. Rahu + Moon is 4th aspected by Saturn or this combination be placed in Saturn's sign in any other house, T.B. is generally the consequence.

16. Mars in 5th, Sun in 7th, Saturn in Aries : the native lives for 70 years.

17. If the 8th lord Mars be in Aries or Leo, the native of this lagna is likely to live for 45 years.

18. For the native of this ascendant, Jupiter in Aries and Mars of Pisces make him live for only 12 years.

19. If Sun + Jupiter + Rahu + Mar's combination be in 5th or 6th house, such native leads a sickly and miserable life.

20. If Mars be in 11th with either Rahu or Ketu — such a native's mother dies early.

21. A week lord of the lagna aspected by a weak Sun — the native becomes prone to committing suicide.

22. Weak Moon in 8th with Saturn makes the native an easy prey to the effects of evil sprits which may even cause him commit suicide.

## G. Libra Ascendant

1. If the lord of 6th house (Jupiter) be placed in 1st house and aspected by malefics the possibility is of the native's death by drowning.

2. If the 4th lord Saturn be together in 8th house with the 8th lord Venus, the native might become afflicted with heart ailments.

3. If Saturn be in 4th house and the Sun in Aquarius : the native may suffer heart attack.

4. Rahu in 4th aspected by malefics and Venus : the lord of the lagna be weak, the native may suffer shooting pain in the heart region.

5. If Venus + Saturn + Jupiter be placed together in a bad house (6th, 8th, 12th) the native may die untimely in an accident.

6. If Moon + Saturn + Jupiter be in the sixth house, the native might become afflicted with leprosy.

7. Exalted Jupiter (in Cancer), Mercury in 5th or 9th house, and a strong lagna lord (Venus) make the native live for 80 years.

8. If the lord of the lagna be in 8th, Moon with malefics in 6th or 8th, the native may hardly cross 58 years of age.

9. If the lagna-lord (Venus) be hemmed between malefics and 7th be also occupied with evil planets with Sun being weak : the native may commit suicide.

## H. Scorpio Ascendant

1. If a malefic be placed in 4th house and the 4th lord Saturn be hemmed between malefics also : heart ailment to the native.

2. If the 4th lord Saturn be with 8th lord Mercury in the 8th house : heart trouble.

3. Rahu in 4th with malefics and the lord of the lagna Mars be weak : the native suffers unbearable pain in the heart region.

4. If Mars + Saturn + Mercury be placed together in bad houses with no favourable aspect on them : the native may meet his untimely death in an accident.

5. If the 1st house be occupied by a malefic and the lagna-lord Mars be weak, the native remains ill despite treatment.

6. If the lord of the lagna (Mars) be placed in 4th and Mercury and Saturn be together in 12th house the native may get afflicted with leprosy.

7. Sun of its own sign in 10th, Saturn in 1st, Moon of Aquarius in 4th and the lagna lord with a benefic in 7th make the native get full age (80 years or beyond)

8. If Sun + Mars + Jupiter + Rahu be in 6th and Venus be in 7th the native remains perpetually ill.

9. Sun in 12th with either Rahu or Ketu makes the native's mother die soon.

# I. Sagittarius Ascendant

1. If the lord of 6th (for this ascendant), Venus, be aspected by malefics, the native may lose his eye-sight due to water.

2. If the lord of 4th, Jupiter be in Capricorn or be combust (*i.e.* with in 12° from The Sun) the native is likely to suffer heart trouble.

3. The same is the consequence if Saturn of Pisces be in 4th, 6th lord Moon and Sun be hemmed between the malefics.

4. A weak Jupiter with Rahu in 4th gives shooting pain in the heart region.

5. If Moon and Venus be together in evil houses with no benefic aspect of Jupiter, the native may meet his or her untimely death in an accident.

6. If for the native of this ascendant Moon, the lord of 8th be in 1st and Jupiter be in 8th, the native remains perpetually ill.

7. If Sun, Mars and Saturn be in the 1st house, even though Jupiter be weak and moon be in 12th, the native may live well beyond 70 years.

8. If there be exchange between Jupiter of Scorpio and Mars of Sagittarius, the native may die at early age.

9. Placement of Saturn in 5th with Rahu may bode ill for the native's mother.

10. Weak moon in 8th house with Saturn may cause the native suffer trouble due to evil sprits.

## J. Capricorn Ascendant

1. For the native of this ascendant if the lord of 6th, Mercury, be placed in 1st house blindness due to water may be the consequence. Such natives must always protect their eyes while going for swimming.

2. Heart ailment will be the consequence if the native has 8th lord, Sun, in 8th house.

3. The same is the consequence if the native has any malefic in 4th or 5th with no redeeming aspect of Jupiter.

4. Shooting pain in the heart region will be the consequences if Sun be hemmed between two malefics for the native of this ascendant.

5. If Saturn, Mars or Sun be together in an adverse house the native may die in an accident.

6. If moon be in 6th of Gemini, all benefics be in 1st, 4th, 7th, 10th houses with no adverse planet in 8th : the native may live for 86 years.

7. Saturn in the lagna (1st house), Moon of Aries in 4th, Mars in 7th and Sun in 10th house with any malefic make the native enjoy kingly opulence but die around 60 years of age.

8. The lord of the lagna (1st house) Saturn be in 8th with malefics, the 8th lord Sun with malefics in 6th with no benefic aspect : the native dies before his attaining 50 years of age.

9. Fourth lord Mars in 12th, Saturn in 7th of Cancer, with 7th lord Moon in 8th make be native die in air crash around 35 years.

10. Placement of Saturn with Rahu or Ketu and Mar's aspect on it make the combination fatal for the native's mother.

11. If the lagna lord Saturn be hemmed between the malefics with 7th also occupied by a malefics and the Sun of weak strength make the native lead a sickly life and commit even suicide in desperation.

12. 6th lord, Mercury, in 7th or 10th; lagna (1st house) aspected by Mars : the native leads a miserable life because of his ailment and enemies.

# K. Aquarius Ascendant

1. 6th lord Moon aspected by Mars or other malefics makes the native suffer danger from water. Such persons must avoid going near big water courses or rivers.

2. Lord of 4th Venus be together with 8th lord Mercury— particularly in 8th house the native becomes prone to suffering from heart trouble.

3. Placement of Saturn in Taurus (in 4th) and of Sun in the lagna itself make the native suffer heart ailment.

4. If Saturn + Venus + Mercury be together in Aquarius in evil houses, the native suffers the danger of dying in an accident.

5. If the lord of lagna (1st house) Saturn be weak by placement or degrees the native remains ill for most of his life. If Saturn be in 8th with Mercury in (8th lord) in 1st house the native doesn't get cured even by treatment.

6. Jupiter in Lagna (going by the dictum : KUMBHE KARKAT VAT) even with malefics makes the native become renowned and rich though he may not survive beyond 60.

7. Saturn in the lagna with any planet; Moon with malefics (count Rahu & Ketu also among them) in 8th or 12th house : the native will be a man with strong character, he shall be a scholar but may not live beyond 56.

8. If Sun, Saturn Mars or Rahu be together in one house- particularly 1st or 12th - the native will lead a miserable life from health's point of view.

9. Second lord Saturn with Rahu or Ketu makes the native's mother die early.

10. A weak sun, lagna or its lord hemmed between malefics with their evil aspect reaching the 1st : such a native may commit suicide.

11. A weak Moon with Saturn makes the native believer in the ghosts or evil spirits which may also cause his death.

# L. Pisces Ascendant

1. The Sixth lord Sun aspected by malefics makes the native suffer from eye-trouble frequently.

2. If 6th lord Sun be affected by malefic aspects and benefics be in 6th or 12th the native may suffer unbearable heart-pain.

3. Saturn of Gemini in 4th and Sun of Aquarius in 12th makes the native suffer heart ailments.

4. Lord of 8th Venus be in 1st, lord of the lagna Jupiter in 8th and a malefic casting a direct aspect on 1st : the native is likely to remain perpetually ill despite undergoing regular treatment for the various ailments.

5. Eighth lord Venus be in 1st, and 1st house itself and Jupiter receiving benefic influences : the native may live for about 100 years.

6. Mars in Cancer in 5th, Sun in 7th and Saturn of Aries : the native lives for 70 years only but in mostly good health.

7. Saturn + Mars in 1st, Moon in 8th and Jupiter in 6th : the native may live only 32 years. The native will live for short age if 2nd or 12th the house be occupied by malefics, lagnesh (lagna-lord) Jupiter weak with 2nd or 12th receiving no benefit aspect.

8. Saturn in 1st, Moon in 4th, Mars in 7th and Sun in 10th with any benefic planet : the native of this ascendant leads a kingly life but expires at 60 due to over-indulgence.

9. Rahu, Venus, Saturn and Sun-together and unaspected by benefics—with the lord of the lagna weak : the native may turn into a patricide (killer of father) but he may himself not survive for long after that.

10. Jupiter + Sun + Rahu + Mars together in 12th and Venus in 7th make the native lead a very miserable and sickness prone life.

11. Saturn in 2nd with Rahu or Ketu is a very had omen for the native's mother.

12. Lord of lagna Jupiter and the lagna itself be hemmed between malefics : the native may came his mother's death in most unseemly circumstances.

# CHAPTER FIVE

# General Rules for Ascertaining Health and Longevity

The rules that govern good health also apply to longevity as well. For nobody would love to live a hundred years long sickly life. But before we lay down the broad rules we would like to acquaint our readers with words 'short' 'medium' and 'long' life as used in the rules given ahead. Generally the ancient technological text categorise them the following way : upto the age of 32—short life; from 32 to 64 - medium life and beyond 64 long. However there is to hard and fast rule about this categorization. A margin of one unit i.e. 6 or 7 or 8 years could be acceptable.

For determining longevity the general rules are :

1. The lord of the eighth in 6th or 12th conjoined with a malefic : the native's life span is short, if the lord of the first is weak.

2. The lord of the eighth in eighth aspected by a benefic : long-life.

3. The lords of the first and eighth together in 6th or 12th from the ascendant (lagna) and aspected by a benefic : long-lived.

4. The lords of the first, eighth and length in a angle or trine or in eleventh (severally or jointly) and aspected by a benefic or benefics : long-life. But if they be weak and conjoined with Saturn : short life.

5. The lords of the 1st, 8th and 10th strong and conjoined with/ aspected by benefics (or benefic) : long life provided they are not conjoined with Saturn. If only two of the above lords fulfil this condition, then medium life; if only one does so : short life.

6. The lord of the 8th posited in an evil house/in a malefic's sign and conjoined with malefic : short life.

7. The lord of the eighth in an angle, trine, third, eighth or eleventh from the ascendant in a benefic's sign, conjoined with/aspected by a benefic : long life.

8. The lord of the 1st in 8th, the lord of the 8th conjoined with/ aspected by a malefic-both combust or in enemy's sign/or 6th short life.

9. The lord of 8th exalted in angle (1st, 4th, 7th or 10th) or trine (5th or 9th) or the lord of 8th in 8th and the lord of the first in first-both conjoined with/aspected by benefics : long life.

10. The lord of the 12th strong in his own sign and aspected by benefics : Long and happy life. In short, for longevity and health/sickness the main point of consideration should be whether the Sun is strong by location and position, conjoined with/aspected by benefics. These solar considerations in any horoscope confer good health and longevity. Contrarily, a weak, ill-placed Sun conjoined with or aspected by malefic produce adverse results.

11. The lord of the 1st in an angle or trine (i.e. in 1st, 4th, 7th, 10th or 4th or 9th houses) or in the 11th well placed in sign/ navamsha (in own sign or exaltation or a benefic friend's sign/navamsha) conjoined with/aspected by a benefic and not conjoined with/aspected by a malefic : healthy, long and prosperous life.

12. The Moon strong in digital strength, well placed and conjoined with/aspected by benefics : healthy and long-lived existence.

13. A conjunction of benefics in the 1st house : a happy combination from health's point of view.

14. All the angles (1, 4, 7, 10) occupied by benefics with mutual aspect from 1st and 7th as also from 4th and 10th : good for health and prosperity. Even a benefic in the 1st aspected by another benefic from 7th is auspicious.

15. If there be malefics in the angle : it is distinctly bad with consequence of ill health and disease. However if a malefic be in its own house it does good for the native's health.

16. If the first house be untenanted and aspected by its own lord or benefics : very good for health of the native. In case a

malefic be aspecting it this combination turns bad for the native's health.

17. Sun in the ascendant particularly in the sign Aquarius gives heart trouble particularly so if aspected by a benefic.

18. Lord of the 6th, the planet tenanting the same or aspecting it, weak and conjoined with/aspected by a malefic : ill health.

19. If the lord of 6th is a benefic in an angle or trine, conjoined with/aspected by a benefic : total freedom from disease, *i.e.* the native may not fall ill and even if he does he will be cured soon.

20. A malefic in the ascendant conjoined with an enemy : wounds on the body or health trouble.

21. Lord of the sixth, if a malefic in the 1st or 8th house aspected by another malefic : the body may receive many wounds or may fall an easy prey to the diseases.

22. Lord of the lagna (ascendant) in 6th, 8th or 12th conjoined with a malefic or aspected by a malefic : sickly and miserable life.

23. Lord of 6th in first conjoined with Rahu or Ketu : the native's body may receive wounds.

24. If Sun or Moon be together in Cancer or Leo the result may be the native suffering from some emaciating or wasting disease.

25. If the lord of the second or Rahu conjoin with the lord of the third : throat disease of long standing.

26. If Mars and Saturn be together in 2nd house some disease in the ear-nose-throat region in which oozing of blood be frequent. However, this won't be the case if the planets be placed in Capricorn sign.

27. If Rahu be in the first house and a conjunction of the lords of the first and third house : fear from poisonous reptiles.

28. Mars and Saturn in 3rd : some long lasting skin trouble including leprosy.

29. If the third lord be conjoined with Mercury and both be aspected by a malefic : throat trouble.

30. If Moon, Venus and the 2nd lord be conjoined together : eye-sight may be damaged.

31. The Sun, Venus and lord of 1st be conjoined in the invisible half[1] of the zodiac : vision gets deteriorated bading possibly to blindness.

32. If the lords of the 1st, 2nd, 7th and 12th be conjoined in the 6th, 8th or 12th from the lagna (ascendant) : May lead to loss of vision. The 2nd lord will give a clue to the cause of it.

33. If the lords of the 5th or 6th houses be conjoined with Venus : loss of vision or much damaged eye sight.

34. If the lord of the third house be placed in 12th : ear disease.

35. If the lord of the third and Mars conjoined in 1st or 8th : ear disease. The same is the consequence if lord of 6th be placed in 12th and aspecting Mars in 8th.

36. If the Moon in 12th aspected by Sun or vice-versa : eye trouble to the native as well as his wife.

37. The native's eye-sight may be damaged if any two of the five planets : Sun, Moon, Mars, Venus or Saturn be conjoined in 2nd, 6th, 8th or 12th house.

38. If the Moon be conjoined with Saturn in 12th from the ascendant : schizophrenia and other kinds of brain troubles.

39. A conjunction of malefics in 3rd, 5th, 9th or 11th, unaspected by any benefic causes ear trouble or deafness.

40. In case the above mentioned combination be receiving aspect from malefic/s the consequence would be the same.

41. Jupiter in ascendant aspected by Saturn in 7th : disease caused by imbalance in the 'vata' humors in the body like gout, rheumatism etc.

42. Mental disease (also include malignant growth in the head region) would be possible if Jupiter in ascendant is aspected by Mars in 7th.

43. If Aries, Taurus or Sagittarius be rising and aspected by malefics : the native may have very ugly teeth.

---

[1] Half of the zodiac from the cusp of the 1st house to the cusp of the 7th is invisible. The other half remains visible.

44. If Aries, Taurus, Leo, Scorpio, Sagittarius, Capricorn or Aquarius be rising and the Sun be in the 1st house aspected by a malefic : the native may be bald or he may face some hair problem.

45. If the owner of the ascending sign (owner of the sign in the 1st house) and the owner of the sign in which Moon is posited- both be hard, naturally malefic planets the native may become bald. [The hard planets naturally are Mars, Saturn, Sun, Rahu or Ketu and if these planets be placed in the lagna or moon signs through the signs be not owned by hard planets even then the effect would be the name.]

46. The Sun in the 5th or 9th aspected by a malefic : eye-sight may get damaged.

47. Mars or Saturn in 5th or 9th not conjoined with or aspected by a benefic : a disease-prone body—particularly so if the malefic in the 5th or 9th is aspected by another malefic.

48. The Sun in 10th aspecting Mars in 4th : hurt by stone or fall from a high point (mountain, hill etc.)

49. If Sun and Moon together be in 1st house in the sign Pisces : fear from drowning.

50. If Saturn be in Cancer aspected by Moon in Capricorn : dropsy particularly in abdominal region.

51. Sun or Mars in 4th aspected by Saturn in 10th : hurt or wound from a sharp edged weapon.

52. Sun and Moon conjoined in 4th aspecting Mars in 10th : wound by weapon.

53. Sun in 4th aspected by Mars in 10th with Mars himself be aspected by Saturn : serious wound by a wooden log or a lathi blow etc. which may cause some head trouble later on.

54. If Mars be aspecting Sun in 10th : fall from a vehicle causing head injury.

55. If 7th house be occupied by malefics : defective teeth or dental ailments.

56. Moon in 2nd or 8th : the body will perspire much though it may scantily be afflicted with any kind of skin ailment. In

case Moon be conjoined with a malefic the sweat smell will be obnoxious. However a benefic's aspect would mitigate the effect considerably.

57. If Mars or Mercury be together in 10th : the body will emit foul odour.

58. If many malefics be conjoined in 8th : many ailments afflicting simultaneously.

59. Mars and Ketu in 4th : fall from a vehicle or while mounting or alighting the steps.

60. Venus afflicted in 7th : Urinary tract obstruction.

# CHAPTER SIX

# Combinations Indicating Various Diseases

1. If Sun, Mars and Saturn be together in 1st house, the native is likely to suffer from jaundice.

2. If an evil planet be placed in 2nd house while its lord be hemmed between the malefics or placed in the debilited sign, the native is likely to have such diseases, afflictions as may disfigure his or her face.

3. If the lords of 10th or 6th placed in 1st house in conjunction with the lord of 2nd, the native will have eye-troubles which may make him or her lose eye-sight.

4. If Moon, Mercury, Sun and Saturn be in 12th house with Mars in any Kendra (1st, 4th, 7th, 10th) house the native's eye sight remains congenitally weak.

5. If the 6th lord be placed in any sign ruled by a fast moving may planet, the native will develop cataract in the eyes early.

6. If the 8th lord or 1st lord be placed in 6th house the native may have trouble in the left eye.

7. Placement of Venus in 6th or 8th house, unaspected by benefics results in the native having trouble in the left eye.

8. If the 2nd lord be aspected by malefics with the 1st lord also placed in bad house, the consequence is eye trouble.

9. Saturn in 2nd aspected by Mars results in the damage to the right eye.

10. Venus in 8th from lagna (1st house) causes the native's eye ooze water perpetually.

11. Lord of 2nd or 12th from Venus be placed in 6th, 8th or 12th houses, the consequence is eye-trouble.

12. Placement of Mars in 12th or Saturn in 2nd results in the left and right eye's damage respectively. Such natives must keep their eyes well protected.

13. Placement of Venus with the lord of 2nd or 12th or its placement in debilited sign in the Navamsha chart causes eye damage.

14. Weak Moon in 12th house makes the native one eyed.

15. Weak Sun (or of debilited sign *i.e.* Libra) also makes the native one eyed.

16. Leo sign in 7th with Moon be aspected by Mars makes the native one-eyed or he or she may lose the sight of one eye.

17. In Capricorn ascendant placement of Sun in Cancer receiving aspect from Mars also makes the native one eyed.

18. If Sun and Moon be in 12th and 6th or vice versa : the husband and wife both one eyed.

19. Placement of Sun, Rahu and Saturn (together) in 2nd may make the native one eyed.

20. If Mercury and Moon be in 2nd house or the lord of the lagna (1st) be in 2nd either the native be born blind or he or she will have very weak vision.

21. If ascendant be Leo with Moon and Sun placed in it the native may be born blind or he will lose his or her vision due to some accident.

22. Rahu and Sun together in 1st house may make the native one eyed or blind.

23. If the lagna lord, with Sun be placed in 6th, 8th or 12th house the person may be born blind.

24. Mars, Moon, Saturn and Sun be in 2nd, 6th, 12th and 8th respectively the native may be born blind.

25. If Saturn and Mars be in 5th or 9th house with Sun eclipsed by Rahu in 1st, the native may be born blind.

26. If Mars and Moon unaspected by any benefic be placed in 6th, 8th or 12th house the native may lose his or her vision while falling from a high building.

27. Jupiter and Moon be together in 6th, 8th or 12th, the native may lose his or her vision due to extreme heat.

28. If Moon and Venus be together in 6th, 8th or 12th house the native may lose his vision due to over indulgence in sex.

29. If the lord of 1st and 2nd house be associated with Sun or Venus and be placed in 6th, 8th or 12th the native may be born blind.

30. One may lose one's vision due to over indulgence in studies if both Mercury and Moon be placed in 6th, 8th or 12th.

31. Sun and Moon, if together be in 3rd house while receiving debilited Saturn's aspect the consequence is blindness.

32. If Sun in 7th house be placed in a sign owned by Saturn, the native may possibly become blind at the middle age.

33. Mars in Aquarius gives the strong possibility of the native losing his or her eye-sight quickly.

34. Mar and Venus — unaspected by benefics — be together in 6th, 8th or 12th the native may suffer from night blindness. In case they be placed in their own signs then this affliction gets considerably mitigated.

35. In Venus, Moon and the 2nd lord be in 1st house the native might suffer night blindness.

36. Placement of Moon and Sun together in 2nd or 12th house also causes night blindness.

37. If the lord of 2nd be placed with Jupiter in 8th house, the native may be dumb or his or her speech be impaired.

38. If Mercury and 6th lord be together placed in lagna the native becomes a drunkard.

39. Jupiter and 6th lord's placement in conjunction in 1st makes the native dumb.

40. If the 2nd lord and Jupiter be together in 6th, 8th or 12th house the native may become dumb due to some accident-

particularly when an adverse Mars be aspecting the combination.

41. If Mercury be in Cancer, Scorpio or Pisces and aspected by Moon with Sun in 4th aspected by malefics : the native may have more nasal sound in his or her voice.

42. If Moon of Taurus be aspected by malefics of the fag end of the sign, the native may become dumb. In case Moon be aspected by Jupiter or Venus then he or she would speak coherently a few years after his birth.

43. If the Moon be at the fag and a sign owned by a malefic, the native becomes dumb particularly if it is receiving no benefic aspect.

44. If the lord of 2nd & 8th be combined and receiving no benefic aspect, the native becomes dumb.

45. Cancer, Scorpio and Pisces are said to be soundless signs. If Mercury be placed in these and aspected by a weak Moon the native may stammer or have other speech defect.

46. The Moon of bright fortnight be placed with Mars in lagna, the native's speech develops defect.

47. Venus in 2nd house with a cruel (Mars, Saturn or Rahu or Ketu) the native will lisp while speaking and his or her vision may also be defective.

48. Despite being well versed and quite learned the native will develop stage-fright and may not be able to speak if the 4th lord be Mars or Saturn placed in 7th house.

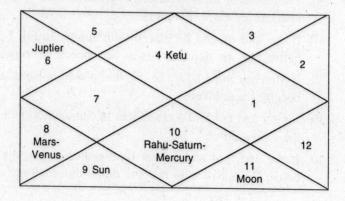

[**Note** : Always go for the position of 2nd lord and the position of Mercury to detect speech defects. See the above Chart. In the above chart the lord of 2nd Sun is placed in adverse house (6th) with the significator of speech Mercury itself is hemmed between two malefics. This person, despite having all pleasures is dumb right since birth.]

49. Rahu in 6th and lord of lagna be in 6th makes the native susceptible to suffering consumption type of diseases like T.B.

50. If Moon's sign (Cancer) be occupied by Mercury, the native suffers from consumptive diseases.

51. Weak or afflicted Venus if be placed with the lagna lord in either 6th, 8th or 12th houses, the native's body becomes prone to suffering consumptive diseases.

52. Mars in 4th house from the ascendant or Moon and Rahu in 12th also makes the native susceptible to consumptive diseases.

53. If Mars or Saturn from adverse house be casting their direct aspect on the 1st house, one becomes asthmatic which later on may develop into tuberculosis (T.B.).

54. Sun in Leo or Cancer be posited with weak moon the consequence is T.B.

55. Mercury in Cancer also makes one prone suffering T.B.

56. Moon placed amidst malefics and Saturn in Aries be in 7th causes pleurisy like ailments.

57. Moon in Cancer or Pisces be in 4th, 10th, 11th or 12th house with Jupiter in 8th causes T.B. which may turn a terminal disease.

58. Venus is 8th aspected by malefics causes diabetes which may lead to other diseases causing the death of the native.

59. If Moon be hemmed between Saturn and Mars, Sun in Capricorn and Rahu be in 7th : the consequence is T.B. likely to be proving fatal.

60. If Sun and Moon be exchanging their signs (*i.e.* Sun be in Cancer and Moon be Leo) the native may get afflicted with

asthma leading to T.B.—particularly if these two planets' position be adverse in the Navamsha chart as well.

61. Mars with Moon be in 6th or 8th and aspected by the lagna lord hemmed between malefics : T.B. of lungs.

62. Sun be in 11th, Saturn in 5th and any malefic in 8th : asthma inducing T.B. eventually.

63. If Sun be in 1st, 4th or 8th with Saturn in 10th alone or alongwith Mars : T.B. of lungs.

64. Sun in Capricorn and Moon be in 8th hemmed between malefics : bronchial ailments of severe type including T.B.

65. If the lagna lord and 6th lord be in 1st, 10th or 6th, 4th with Saturn, Rahu or Ketu the native becomes immobile due to some wasting disease.

66. If Jupiter or Mars be either in 1st or 7th with a weak Moon in 6th, 8th or 12th the native may become afflicted with a severe mental ailment. However, the aspect on them from a strong lagna lord may give the hope of cure from that disease.

67. If there be an association by aspect or conjunction or exchange between Saturn and Mars with either of them aspecting 9th, 5th or 7th house, the native may gradually become mad or demented.

68. Saturn in 12th with a weak moon leads to lunacy, but a benefic's aspect (Jupiter's) may mitigate the effect.

69. If Taurus and Sagittarius signs be occupied by malefics the native may have some problem related to his hair.

70. Moon in Cancer aspected by Mars which the ascendant he Leo, Sagittarius, Scorpio or Virgo—the native may become bald due to some infection.

71. Mars be placed with a weak Moon unaspected by any benefic causes blood related ailments including drastic fluctuation in the blood pressure.

72. Rahu in Lagna and Moon in 6th house may cause epilepsy to the native.

73. If the lord of the ascendant (lagna) be placed in 4th or 12th house with either Mars or Mercury, the native may get afflicted with leprosy.

74. Leprosy may afflict the native if Jupiter be in 6th house in conjunction with either Saturn or Mars.

75. Mar in the ascendant, Sun in 8th and Saturn in 4th make the native suffer from leprosy.

76. If Mars or Saturn be either in 2nd or 12th house, Moon in 1st and Sun in 7th cause leucoderma or even leprosy.

77. Lord of lagna (1st house) in 8th and hemmed between the malefics causes leprosy.

78. Jupiter in 8th, Mars in 6th alongwith either Saturn or Mercury and 1st house be receiving direct aspect from a malefic : the consequence is leprosy with red spots.

79. Hard or evil planets be placed in Cancer, Pisces or Scorpio signs with no benefic planet aspecting them : leprosy is the result. It may be of that deadly variety in which knee to feet part of the leg gets wasted, making the person lame.

80. If Moon with Venus be aspected by malefics and placed together in Cancer, Scorpio or Pisces together in Cancer, Scorpio or Pisces sign the consequence is perpetual itching sensation culminating into white-patched leprosy.

81. If Saturn, Mars, Moon and Venus be together and receiving aspect from malefics the native may suffer from oozing type of leprosy.

82. If the 6th lord be placed in 1st house with the Sun the native may suffer from leprosy.

83. If the lord the lagna be placed with Mars, Moon and Rahu or Ketu, leprosy is the result.

84. If the lord of the lagna, lord of the 6th be Mercury and placed in conjunction with Saturn or Rahu the native may get afflicted with some very painful skin disease like leprosy.

85. If 6th lord be Jupiter and placed with Venus aspected by malefic the native may get afflicted with leprosy like disease in the mouth.

86. If Mars be together with the lagna lord, the native may inherit father's skin disease or defect.

The following six planetary combination in a horoscope are indicative of mental derangement and insanity.

87. Jupiter in the ascendant with Mars or Saturn (or both) are in the 7th house.

88. Saturn in the ascendant with Mars in the 5th or the 9th house.

89. Saturn and weak Moon in the 12th house.

90. Moon and combust (with in about 10° from the Sun) in the ascendant.

91. Very weak Moon (in digital as well as positional strength) occupying 1st, 5th or 9th house in conjunction with a malefic planet.

92. When a benefic planet occupies the 8th house and, Rahu, the weak Moon and another malefic planet occupy the 12th house in conjunction.

93. The Sun in the 12th house, Saturn in ascendant and either the Moon or Mars in 5th or 9th with no aspect of a benefic planet on either of them.

94. If the Sun is in the 1st, the 5th or the 9th and Jupiter is in the 3rd or in one of the Kendra (1st, 4th, 7th, 10th) house and also if the birth takes place on Saturday or Tuesday.

Leucoderma is said to manifest under the following eight planetary combination.

95. If the lord of the ascendant and Mercury are together in conjunction with Rahu or Ketu, or if the Moon and Mars are so placed.

96. When Moon occupies Aries or Taurus with Saturn and Mars.

97. Saturn and Mars in the 2nd or 12th and Sun and Moon in 7th (Tula) or 1st (Aries) signs.

98. If the Sun and the Moon, in conjunction of Mars, Saturn or Rahu, occupy Cancer, Scorpio or Pisces.

99. When the Moon, Venus and malefics including the Sun occupy watery signs like Cancer, Scorpio or Pisces.

100. When the Sun, Saturn, Mars and Moon respectively occupy the 7th, 12th, 2nd or 1st house.

101. When the lord of the ascendant occupies the 8th house in conjunction with or aspected by strong malefics as also the lord of 8th.

102. When Moon occupies 4th house and is aspected by Venus. In all these cases the diseases manifest as white-patched leucoderma if the Moon and Rahu occupy the ascendant with no conjunction with the lord of the ascendant. It turns out to be dark patched one if the Moon and Saturn conjoin the ascendant.

Consider the following chart of a young lady who became a victim of leucoderma. But due to medicines and prompt propitiation of the adverse planets she was cured.

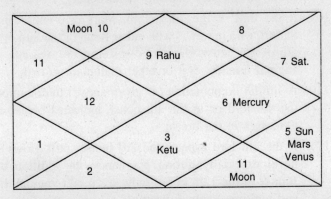

A debilited Mercury with Rahu in 1st caused her this trouble but Moon and Jupiter's mental aspect provided the redeeming feature and cured her.

The following planetary combinations cause various disease attacking the native simultaneously. In other words they make the native disease prone.

103. When the lords of the ascendant and 6th mutually and fully aspect each other.

104. When Moon occupies the 5th or 6th house; Sun occupies the ascendant and the lord of the ascendant is in conjunction with any strong malefic.

105. When Saturn, Sun and Moon are aspected by Mars or conjoined with Rahu.

106. Sun and Moon together in Leo or Cancer induces consumptive disease like phthisis.

107. Phthisis or connected disease is the consequence when Saturn is aspected by Sun or Mars in the 6th house and Rahu in 7th house from Saturn and Saturn itself be receiving no foul aspect from any strong planet.

## Some Combination for Diseases in Female Natives

108. When the 2nd house is not strong enough, the ascendant is occupied by Saturn which, in turn, is aspected either by Mars or the Sun, the native suffers from small-pox with marks showing on her face. Pimples and other mark and spots also occur on the face marring facial beauty.

109. If the lord of the 7th or 5th, Mars or Venus aspected by Saturn, who in turn is with either Rahu or the Sun or occupies 5th or 7th house, the native suffers from ovarian, womb or vaginal tumour, cyst or other malignant growth.

110. A similar combination (as given above) in conjunction with the 4th lord or in the 4th house indicates breast cancer or abscesses in the breast.

111. If the 6th lord aspects the 3rd house, puss flows from the navel especially during pregnancy. In addition to above, Jupiter in the 12th house indicates secret vaginal discharges and multiple vaginal diseases.

## Cancer Inducing Planetary Combinations

112. If any two signs from Cancer, Scorpio, Pisces, Capricorn and Libra signs be under the influence of the lord of 6th, 8th or 12th, cancer may develop.

113. When Saturn and Mars, either alone or conjoined, respectively, by Ketu and Rahu, are placed in the signs owned by Saturn or Mars, cancer may develop.

114. If the sign Cancer happen to be in 6th house and is occupied by Mars and Saturn or Saturn is in the 7th house therefrom, the native may be afflicted with cancer. (disease)

115. If Mars and Saturn are placed in mutual Kendra (1, 7 or 4th, 10th) houses owned by their natural enemies or in conjunction with Sun and Moon respectively, a malignant growth in the body could be feared.

116. When the lord of the ascendant and of the 4th house are placed in the 6th house in combustion or retrogression and either of them/both of them are aspected by Saturn and Mars, cancer (disease) may manifest itself.

Consider the following horoscope where a strong Saturn aspected by stronger Mars caused cancer in penis and its subsequent amputation.

### Lagna Chart

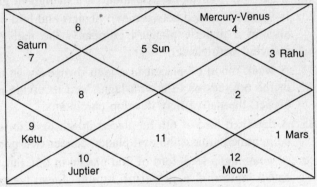

### Navamsha Chart

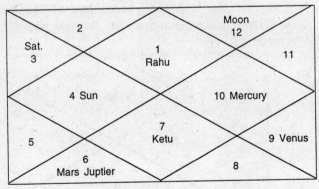

Mark that intrinsic strength of the good planets in hardly better in Navamsha chart as well.

117. When Mars and Saturn be aspecting each other with no redeeming benefic aspect.

118. Rahu and Saturn's placement in a bad house also induces maliqnant growth in the native's body.

119. Saturn and Mars position in 6th or 8th alongwith either Rahu or Ketu : the native may suffer from carcinoma (cancer).

120. If lord of 2nd be in 8th and the 8th lord along with Moon be in 6th, 8th or 12th house the native may suffer from leukemia (blood-cancer)

121. If Sun be in 6th, 8th, 12th house with evil planets the native may suffer of carcinoma of the intestines or peptic ulcer of the stomach.

122. Rahu with Sun in 1st also induces a malignant growth.

123. If Sun be hemmed between evil planets and lord of lagna be also in a malefic planet's company, the native may get afflicted with cancer.

124. A weak moon be placed in a sign owned by an evil planet or the 6th, 8th or 12th with lagna lord receiving no benefic aspect, the native may develop carcinoma.

125. A debilited lord of 6th be placed in 8th or 12th with Moon be hemmed amidst the evil planet, cancer will be the result.

126. A weak lagna lord, lord of 2nd placed in 6th, 8th, 12th may cause cancer if a powerful Jupiter doesn't aspect lagna (ascendant).

Consider the following horoscope of the person who developed leukemia and despite the best possible treatment couldn't survive.

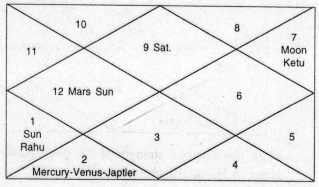

(In the chart given above). The ascendant is occupied by a malefic (Saturn) and the ascendant lord Jupiter is in 6th (house of disease) with the 6th lord. The 7th lord Mercury is also adversely placed in 6th Sun and Moon both are afflicted with the association of Rahu and Ketu.

127. If the lord of lagna Mercury be placed in the signs owned by Mars, the native have a possibility of developing mouth-cancer.

128. Mars and sun together in 2nd house may cause a severe mouth affliction.

129. If Venus be posited in Cancer or Aries, no matter which house it is placed in, the native will emit foul smell from his or her mouth.

130. Moon in 1st and the 6th lord Mercury also give the native a foul smelling mouth.

131. If Venus be in Capricorn and Aquarius (in the signs owned by Saturn) the native's mouth will give foul smell.

132. Mercury in 6th and Moon and Venus in Aries give the native a foul smelling month.

133. If the sign in 1st house be either Taurus, Aries or Sagittarius and the ascendant be aspected by malefics : foul smelling mouth due to dental problem.

134. If malefics be in 7th unaspected by benefics , the native may suffer dental diseases.

135. If Moon, Saturn and Sun be in 7th house unaspected by benefics : the native may lose his or her teeth early.

136. If Rahu be posited in the second house from the house occupied by the lord of 7th : the native may have weak and protruded teeth.

137. Rahu in 5th or 1st also gives big and ugly teeth.

138. If the 6th lord be posited with Rahu the native will lose his or her teeth in the major period of the 6th lord.

139. 6th lord's association with 2nd lord also makes the teeth weak. The native will lose his or her teeth in the major period of either the 6th or the 2nd lord.

140. Jupiter in 1st house with Rahu also causes chronic teeth trouble.

141. Rahu alone in second house in the sign owned by Mars makes the native have big, ugly and weak teeth.

142. The native may be addicted to drugs if 12th lord he posited in its debilited sign.

143. The native may become addicted to drugs or liquor if the lagna lord be in its debited sign or in the sign owned by its enemy.

144. Malefics in 12th house causes addiction to drugs.

145. Jupiter of its debited sign in any house makes the native infatuated to drugs and liquor.

146. A weak Jupiter and debited lagna lord may make native ruin his or her health because of drug addiction.

147. If Mars be the lagna lord aspected by Saturn without Jupiter's aspect may make native ruin his health and life due to some secret addiction.

148. If Sun, Mars and Saturn be together in 6th, the native may become lame.

149. Saturn and 12th lord, both, he posited in 12th itself : the native may lose its one feet due to some ailment.

150. If the lord of 8th house and the lord of 9th be together in 4th house the native may have his or her legs severely hurt, as much as to makes him lame.

151. If Moon and Saturn be posited together in any of the following signs : Pisces, Scorpio, Aries, Cancer or Capricorn — particularly in 5th or 9th : the native may become lame due to some accident in water.

152. If Moon and Saturn be in cancer sign unaspected by any benefic, the native may become lame. Or, his or her leg may be severely hurt.

153. If Saturn and Venus be together in any sign unaspected by benefic planet or devoid of any benefic influence, the native may become lame or have his or her one of the legs incapacitated.

154. Seventh lord be posited together with Saturn the native may become lame as a result of some accident.

155. If the Moon be in 4th with its being unaspected by benefics even in the Navamsha Chart the native may develop some serious trouble in his or her throat region.

156. Saturn and Mars conjunction in 6th, 12th — unaspected by benefic : elephantitis or a similar ailment may trouble the native.

157. If Saturn, Mars, Mercury and Jupiter be posited in the same sign and Venus be in 4th: the possibility is that the native's hands or legs may be amputed.

158. If malefics be in the Kendra houses and Jupiter, unaspected by any benefic be in 5th, the native may develop a severe affliction in his or her thigh region. The same is the consequence of Mars, being the 6th lord, placed in the 3rd house.

159. The native's gait may be adversely affected if the lord of the lagna be placed in 12th with Mars.

160. The same is the consequence if the following combinations occur in the native's horoscope :

    (a) if the 9th lord and 8th lord be placed in Capricorn, Aquarius or Pisces sign.

    (b) Mars and Moon be together in 6th and the native be born on the full moon day.

    (c) Saturn Mars and Moon be congruent in 12th house.

161. If Saturn be in lagna aspected by a malefic the native may get a severe blow in his heed.

162. If Saturn, Moon and Mars be in 12th house together the native may have his thighs weak and the joint fragile.

## Combinations for Cancer Affliction

163. If the lord of the 6th, 8th and 12th house from the Sun sign be associated with Rahu or Ketu, the possibility of cancer affliction is very much there.

164. The natives of cancer ascendant are normally prone to getting afflicted with cancer. If Saturn, Mars and Jupiter be associated

with the lords of the 6th, 8th and 12th houses the native may have cancer affliction.

165. If Mars and Saturn be aspecting each other in the association of Rahu and Ketu, the native may have cancer affliction.

166. Saturn, Mars and Rahu be together in 6th, 8th or 12th and receiving adverse aspects, the possibility of cancer afflicting the native gets more pronounced.

167. If the lord of 2nd be in 8th, and the lord of 8th be in the lagna with Moon, or 6th, 8th or 12th lord he aspecting Mars, the native may have leukemia.

168. If the lord of the 6th, 1st or 10th be posited with evil planets, the native may become afflicted with cancer.

169. If the Sun be posited with the 6th, 12th or 8th lord, the native may become afflicted with carcinoma of intestines or stomach. The presence of Rahu may accentuate the affliction.

170. An adverse Sun posited with the 6th lord makes cancer affliction more than a likely possibility.

171. A weak Moon in the sign owned by evil planets — particularly in 6th, 8th or 12th house may cause cancer affliction.

172. If the Moon be aspected by Saturn or Mars simultaneously, the native becomes prone to getting afflicted with cancer or any fatal and incurable disease.

173. If an evil planet be in 2nd house with 2nd lord afflicted with an evil aspect and be in association with the 6th, 8th or 12th lord : the native may have cancer like incurable disease.

174. If the lagna (1st house) be occupied by an evil planet, the lord of 6th be Jupiter or associated with the 6th lord with the luminaries also afflicted by the evil planets' effect, the native may have blood cancer. Consider the following horoscope which fulfils these condition. The native developed leukemia and after six month's treatment by radiation therapy, expired due to incurability of the deadly disease.

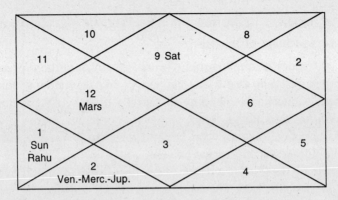

175. The lord of the lagna be in 6th with evil planets with a very weak moon afflicted by the lord of 2nd or 7th house : the consequence is cancer.

176. If Moon be posited with evil planets in 8th, 6th lord be in 12th associated with the Sun, and lord of lagna be afflicted with evil planets the native may develop cancer but will survive. Consider the following horoscope.

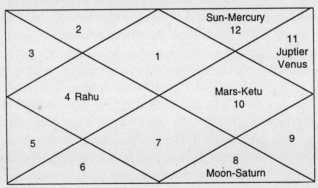

Despite the horoscope fulfilling the condition described above, the native, a lady whose private part got afflicted with cancer could survive only because the lord of the lagna, Mars is getting directional strength and being in the exalted sign, Capricorn, and also getting additional strength with the association of Ketu.

177. A weak 7th lord in 8th unaspected by benefic planets and associated with malefics might result in cancer of the private part if the 6th lord be also afflicted.

## Astrological indicators for detecting the possibility of having carcinomous affliction

Cancer is an abnormal type of growth in a tissue of susceptible organ or it may due to destructive type like ulceration which does not heal. Cancer can manifest in various organs like pituitary, brain, skin, thyroid, throat, lungs, stomach, esophagus, uterus, prostate etc. Astrologically cancer can be anticipated in a native's horoscope if the Sun or the Moon, the 6th, 8th house or the 12th house and their lords of the Zodiacal signs like Virgo-Pisces, Cancer, Scorpio and Libra are afflicted. The 6th house primarily indicates disease and the 8th, a chronic disease. Since cancer has a tendency to run a chronic course, their usually exists a relationship between the 6th and 8th houses or their lords. Saturn and Rahu are indicators of chronic disease. So, they have a major role to play in these disease. Mars is associated with ulcerative type of growths or those that require dissection. The Rahu-Ketu axis may influence the afflicting planets, the 6th or the 8th lords or the houses. The afflicting planets can be Saturn, Palm, Ketu, Mars and the 6th, 8th or the 12th lords. Deep seated, indiagnosable tumours well have the sign Scorpio afflicted. Restricted, localised and well defined growths may have the influences Saturn or other afflicting planets. Fast disseminating cases will have usually afflicted watery signs. The onset of the disease will be likely during the period of the afflicted planets, weak and afflicted 6th or 8th lords or the period of a Badhaka lord placed in a badhaka house. If the sub-periods following the ones which caused the disease are of benefics, favourable lords or Yogakarakas the disease may be diagnosed early and treated. The transit of Saturn or Rahu over the malefic Dasa lords, the 6th or the 8th lords or natal Saturn or Rahu may initiate the disease. If there is influence of benefics over the above said initiators, from a strong position the disease may get completely cured.

What holds true for cancer also holds true for AIDS, though this latest affliction must have the lagnesh (lord of the lagna) weak with a very weak moon.

A strong lagna lord, the Moon and the Sun also help in quick relief. To find out which organ is likely to be afflicted, we rely on the assignment of various organs to different Zodiacal signs and houses, and the Ascendant and planets. Let us enumerate a few of them from the point of view of detection of cancer.

(i) *Brain, structures of the central nervous system*, pituitary etc : 1st house, Aries, the Sun, Mercury, Jupiter.

(ii) *Facial organs, mouth, jaw etc* : 2nd house, Taurus, Venus.

(iii) *Throat, thyroid, epiglottis* : 2nd, 3rd, 11th houses, Taurus, Venus and the Sun.

(iv) *Blood and related structure* : the Moon, Mars, the Sun.

(v) *Lymphatics*—the Moon.

(vi) *Skin* : Capricorn, the Sun, Saturn, Mercury.

(vii) *Eye* : 2nd, 12th house, the sun, the moon, Venus.

(viii) *Ear, Nasal structures* : 3rd, 11th house, Gemini, Aquarius, Mercury.

(ix) *Lungs and bronchial structures* : 3rd house, Gemini, Mercury, the Moon.

(x) *Abdomen* : 4th, 5th, 6th, 8th houses; Virgo, the Moon, the Sun, Mercury, Saturn.

(xi) *Male Sexual Organs* : 7th, 8th houses, Scorpio, Venus, Mars.

(xii) *Female Sexual Organs* : 5th, 7th, 8th houses; Libra, Scorpio, Venus, Mars, the Moon.

(xiii) *Urinary System* : 7th house, Libra, Venus, the Moon.

(xiv) *Breasts.* 4th house, Cancer, the Moon.

(xv) *Bones and Ligaments* : 3rd, 11th, 12th houses Capricorn, the Sun, Saturn.

Apart from studying these combinations in the natal (lagna) Chart, the Navamsha chart should also be studied to know the strength or weaknesses of the concerned planets.

## Broad Principles for Disease Detection

(a) Either one or both the luminaries (the Sun as the Moon) will be afflicted in the natal or Navamsha Chart.

(b) Malefics like Rahu, Saturn and Mars have a major role in causing and advancing the disease.

77

(c) Benefics like Jupiter Mercury, Venus, if unafflicted, well-placed and with a good lordship, influencing the Dasa lords or afflicting planets help in early diagnosis and cure.

(d) The Zodiacal signs indicating the concerned organs will usually be afflicted by natural or functional malefics.

(e) Badhakas and planets in Badhaka houses play a vital role.

(f) A strong lagna lord, the influence of benefics on the 6th, 8th or 12th lords, the Sun and the Moon, help in early diagnosis and cure. Along with medical treatment, which include, surgery, radiotherapy and chemotherapy, proper remedies like Japa, Homa and gem therapy related to the afflicted planet are to be performed. By performing remedial measures at the earliest when such factors are present can even prevent the onset of cancer.

Having given in nut shell the various combination that give rise to certain physical and mental affliction, we shall now be discussing the remedial measures for propitiating various adverse planets alongwith some of the medical hints for achieving a cure of them.

# CHAPTER SEVEN

# Planetary Afflictions and Their Remedial Measures

Of course the course of destiny can't be altered yet efforts could be made to mitigate the adverse conditions arising in our tryst with destiny. Remedial measures to alleviate afflicted periods of planets have the sanction of great astrologers of the past, of the authors of Dharma Shashtras and experience. Given below are some of the tried and tested methods to propitiate adverse or evil planets.

## Proportion of Various Planets

(a) **The Sun** : Ruby of five and quarter 'rattis' should be worn in a gold finger which is to be worn in the right ring finger if the sun be posited in 1st to 7th house and in the left ring finger if the sun be posited in 7th to 12th houses in the natal (lagna) Chart. Apart from it, keeping fast on Sundays and ending it at the sun-set after worshipping the deity sun will also be useful. Wear the ring on Sunday at sun-rise hour.

(b) **The Moon** : Pearl is the gem for propitiating the Moon. Wearing a pearl of minimum three and half rattis in the first finger (right if the moon be in 1 to 7th house and in the left if it be in 8th to 12 houses) on Monday at the day-break and worshipping the deity Lord Shiv will also help. Keeping fast on Mondays and eating only white coloured eatables propitiates the Moon quickly.

(c) **Mars** : Mars is to be propitiated by wearing a coral embedded ring in gold or silver ring. Wear it on Tuesday at sun-rise after worshipping the deity Lord Hanuman. Those who keep fast on this day skip their lunch and breakfast and end their fast at sun-set. Visiting the temple of Lord Hanuman also brings good results.

**79**

(*d*) **Mercury** : The deity to be propitiated for adverse Mercury is Lord Vishnu. The gem to be worn in a gold finger is emerald. Normally fast is not observed on this day (Wednesday) though donating green things (objects of green colour/shade) brings quick relief.

(*e*) **Jupiter** : Topaj (or yellow sapphire or Pokharaj) is recommended for wearing it in a gold or silver ring depending upon its relationship in the natal chart with the luminaries. The deity to be propitiated is Lord Ganesh. Keeping fast on Thursdays is highly beneficial.

(*f*) **Venus** : Wearing a diamond of five and quarter rattis in a gold or silver ring or even in platinum is recommended. The deity to be worshipped is Goddess Bhagwati (Devi) or Lord Shiv. Keeping fasts on Fridays and eating no sour eatables is greatly helpful. Wearing shinning white clothes for those having adverse Venus causing semen related diseases is found to be quite effective to do the needful.

(*g*) **Saturn** : Giving as alms black objects, mustard oil and wearing 'Neelam' (blue sapphire) in silver are the necessary remedial measures. Worshipping Lord Hanuman and keeping fast will also help.

(*h*) **Rahu** : The gem to be worn in a silver or gold ring is 'Gomed'. The deity to be worshipped is Lord Shiv. Lighting a lamp at the sun-set in a Shiv-temple is also recommended.

(*i*) **Ketu** : The gem is 'Cat's eye' or as it is called is North India 'Lehasunia'. It is to be worn in a silver ring. The deity to be propitiated is Lord Skanda or Kartikeya.

Apart from these, planets in each sign have different deities who should be propitiated. These details have been culled from various ancient texts which are believed to have successfully withstood the test of time.

1. *The Sun :* From Aries onwards respectively, the deities governing the Sun are Siva, Yakshi, Vishnu, Sarpa, family deity. Vishnu, Bhadrakali, Swayambhu, Gandharva Yaksha, Ayyappa, Pisacha, Kirata.

2. *The Moon :* In Aries and Scorpio — Chamundi; In Taurus— Yakshi; In Libra —Dharmadaiva; In Mercury's houses, Vimana

Sundara and Sundari; In his own house, Sarpa and Dharmadaiva; In Leo—Bhagavati; In Jupiter's houses—Akasa Gandharva; In Saturn's house—spirits and demons.

3. *Mars* : In Aries, Bhuta Rakshasa, Brahma Rakshasa; In Scorpio—Narabhojini, Bala Prabhakshini; In Venus' houses—Bhairava, Yaksha; In Gemini—Narasimha and Gandharva; In Virgo—Narasimha and Yakshi; In Cancer-Bhagavati, Krishna, Chamundi; In Leo—Shiva Bhutas; In Sagittarius—Sasta; In Pisces—Virabhadra; In Saturn's houses—Abhichara Devas.

4. *Mercury* : In Venus, Gandharva; In his own, Gandharva, Kinnara; In Cancer, Jala Pisacha; In Leo, Nagakanya; In Jupiter's, Chamundi; In Saturn's Kavachi, Sula Pisacha, Kala Pisachi.

5. *Jupiter* : In Mars' houses, Siva Bhutas, Durdevata; In Venus', Apasmara Yakshi, Yaksha; In Mercury's, Devata (Yama?); In Cancer and Leo, Devata Gandharva; In Saturn's houses, Bheema Pisacha, Jala Pisacha, Adhama Gandharva.

6. *Venus* : In Mars' houses, Siva Bhutas, Yaksha Rakshasa; In his own and in Cancer, Yaksha, Yakshi; In Mercury's Abhichara Devata; In Leo, Yakshi; In Sagittarius, Murti; In Pisces-Durga; In Capricorn—Apasmara; In Aquarius—Kala Pisacha.

7. *Saturn* : In Aries, Apasmara Devata; In Scorpio, Siva Bhuta; In Taurus, Apasmara Yaksha, Yakshi; In Libra, Bhutanatha(Siva); In Gemini, Vanadevata; In Virgo, Preta; In Cancer, Chandra Devata; In leo, Sasta, Kirata, Pisacha; In Jupiter's houses, Gandharva; In his own houses, Preta and Pisacha.

The 4th house and its lord indicate the family deity. The deities to be propitiated for relieving or controlling planetary afflictions are many. These are : The Sun—Saiva Bhuta; *the Moon*—Durga, Dharma Daivata; *Mars*—Subrahmanya, Bhairva; *Mercury*, Gandharva, Yaksha; *Jupiter*—Devas; *Venus*—Yaksha, Brahimaraksasa; *Saturn*—Sasta, Kirata, Pancha Bhutas; *Rahu* -Naga : *Ketu*—Chandala Devata; *Gulika*—Preta.

## Propitiatory Rites

Add the longitude of the lord of Lagna to that of the lord of the 6th. Note which planet is there or which one is aspecting it. This gives a clue to the propitiatory rite called for, as follows : *The Sun*—

Aghora Bali; *the Moon*—Kapala Homa; *Mercury*—Chakra Home; *Jupiter*—Pratikara Bali; *Mars*—Bhutamaranabali, Khadga Ravanabali, Krittikabali; *Venus*—Pratikarabali, Bhutamaranabali; *Saturn*—Pratikarabali.

## Mantras

The Mantras to be recited for the various planets are many. For the sake of convenience we give a few : *The Sun*-Raja Shyamala; *The Moon*—Bhuvaneswari; *Mars*—Baglamukti; *Mercury*—Tripura Sundari; *Jupiter*—Tara; *Venus*—Kamala; *Saturn*—Dakshina Kali; *Rahu*—Chinna Mata; *Ketu*—Dhumavati. The Mantras of these deities have to be received at the time of initiation from a competent Guru.

## Ramayana to the Rescue

**Srimad Ramayana** of Valmiki has brought untold happiness to millions of persons. Certain chapters are said to be an antidote to certain kinds of afflictions. Some of these have been tried by us and we vouchsafe the fruitfulness of these propitiatory rites. We give the Sargas (cantos, chapters) of this sacred text and as authorised in **Uma Samhita**, state what they can do :

1. Successful performance of righteous activities—*Ayodhya Kanda*, Cantos 21 to 25. Naivedya (offering): 5 bananas.

2. Acquisition of wealth—*Ayodhya*, 32, Naivedya : 5 bananas.

3. Marriage—*Bala Kanda*, 73. For forty days. Naivedya: fresh milk.

4. Final emancipation—*Aranya*, 65 to 68. 5 bananas.

5. For ill-health—*Yuddha*, 59. Honey and milk.

6. Possession by spirits—*Sundara*, 3. Sugar Pongal.

7. Mental Aberration—*Sundara*, 13. Cooked black gram.

8. Poverty—*Sundara* 15. 5 bananas.

9. Sorrow—*Yuddha*. 116. 5 bananas.

10. Calamities— *Yuddha*, 18-19. Coconut.

11. For happy return of a relative—*Sundara*, 36. Mango or Panasa.

12. Bad dreams—*Sundara*, 27. Sugar.

13. For disservice [i.e., atoning for it] to Sri Rama—*Sundara,* 38.5 bananas.

14. All-round happiness in the life to come—*Yuddha.* 13 Pongal with moong dal.

15. For begetting a child—*Bala,* 15-16. Payasam.

16. Easy delivery—*Bala,* 18. Any available object.

17. Fear of imprisonment—*Yuddha,* 117. Any object.

18. For a healthy mind to the children—*Ayodhya,* 1-2. 5 bananas.

19. Successful achievement of all desires—*Bala,* 75-76. Payasa and papad.

20. Favour from superiors—*Ayodhya,* 100. 5 bananas.

21. For health—*Yuddha,* 105 (*Aditya Hridayam*).

The Vimshottari Dasa and Antardasas, if they are malefic, are effectively brought under control by certain chapters (Sargas) of *Sundara Kanda* in **Valmiki Ramayana.** We give some that we have tried with success :—

(1) *The Moon* Dass—Sarga 5; (2) *Mars — Jupiter's Bhukti*-57; (3) *Mars-Venus* — 53; (4) *Rahu-Saturn* — 47; (5) *Rahu-Venus* — 65; (6) *Jupiter* Dasa — 1; (7) *Saturn-Saturn* — 48; (8) *Jupiter-Ketu* — 61-62; (9) *Saturn-Mercury* — 54; (10) *Saturn-Venus* — 38. (11) Mercury Dasa — 35. (12) *Mercury - Ketu* — 15; (13) *Mercury-Mars* — 23; (14) *Ketu-Venus* — 65; (15) *Venus* Dasa — 38.

## Nakshatra Deities

The afflicted Nakshatra too needs propitiation. We have texts dealing with Graha Makha and Nakshatra Makha. The deities of the Nakshatra starting from Aswini and ending with Revati are :

Nasatyas (Aswinis), Yama or Vivasvan, Agni, Brahma, Soma, Rudra, Aditi, Brihaspati, Sarpa-Rudra, Maghavan or Pitris, Bhaga, Aryaman, Savita, Tvashta, Marutvan, Indragni, Mitra, Indra, Nirriti-Rudra, Apam Napat, Visvedevas, Vishnu, Vasus, Varuna, Aja Ekapat, Ahurbudhnya and Pushan.

## Medico-Astro-Numerological Measures

There are various therapies that are available to treat the afflictions. In this subsection we are combining astro-medico-numerological measures. These medical measures are based on the theory that bio-chemical salts have a direct bearing upon the twelve zodiacal signs. So if you are born in a particular period your body suffers a natural deficiency of certain salts. The theory is that if you take these salts regularly you can keep on rejuvenating your body's vitality. This study is particularly confined to bio-chemical measures since these have been detected a definite co-relation between the twelve zodiacal signs and the twelve biochemical salts. Since each sign has a direct bearing upon a particular organ of the body these salts also develop a marked relation with them. The two studies have been combined after a great deal of research and practical experience. Added in the list of the various Ayurvedic Bhasm which are to be used as the tonic to tone up the various parts of the body.

All this does not mean that an affliction brought on by the planet scan be cured only by the remedial measures already suggested or are given in the chart given ahead. Our ancient shave prescribed Mani (precious stones), Mantras and Aushadhi (medicine) jointly. Graha Japa hastens the process of recovery only when the horoscopes assure longevity. It is the combination of all the four remedial measures that assures the best results.

# MEDICO-ASTRO-NUMEROLOGICAL CHART

| If you are born between | Zodiac sign and its owner | Lucky month | Zodiac sign related to | Bio-chemic birth salt | Planet's lucky metal | Ayurvedic bhasim of | Lucky stone | Colour favourable (Chromo-therapy) | Lucky Number | Lucky Days |
|---|---|---|---|---|---|---|---|---|---|---|
| 21.3 to 20.4 | Aries-Mars | Sept. | Head | Kali Phos. | Copper | Coral | Coral | Yellow | 9 | Tuesday |
| 21.4 to 20.5 | Taurus-Venus | June | Throat | Natrum-Sulpha | Zinc | Diamond | Diamond | Indigo Blue | 6 | Friday |
| 21.5 to 20.6 | Gemini-Mercury | May | Chest | Kali Meer | Mercury | Emerald | Emerald | Green | 5 | Wednesday |
| 21.6 to 20.7 | Cancer-Moon | Feb./Jul/Nov. | Heart | Calc. Phos | Silver | Pearl | Pearl | Orange | 2 & 7 | Monday |
| 21.7 to 20.8 | Leo-Sun | Jan./Oct. | Stomach | Mag. Phos. | Gold | Ruby | Ruby | Red | 4 | Sunday |
| 21.8 to 20.9 | Virgo-Mercury | May | Intestines | Kali Sulph | Mercury | Emerald | Emerald | Green | 5 | Wednesday |
| 21.9 to 20.10 | Libra-Venus | June | Kidney | Natrum Sulph | Zinc | Diamond | Diamond | Indigo Blue | 6 | Friday |
| 21.10 to 20.11 | Scorpio-Mars | Sept. | Genital organ | Calc Sulph. | Copper | Coral | Coral | Yellow | 9 | Tuesday |

85

**Medico-Astro-Numerological Chart (*Continued*)**

| If you are born between | Zodiac sign and its owner | Lucky month | Zodiac sign re-lated to | Bio-chemic birth salt | Planet's lucky metal | Ayurvedic bhasim of | Lucky stone | Colour favourable (Chromo-therapy) | Lucky Number | Lucky Days |
|---|---|---|---|---|---|---|---|---|---|---|
| 21.11 to 20.12 | Sagittarius-Juptier | Mar./Dec. | Thighs | Silica | Tin | Topaz | Topaz | Blue | 3 | Thursday |
| 21.12 to 20.1 | Capricorn-Saturn | August | Knee | Calc Phos. | Iron | Blue Sapphire | Blue Sapphire | Violet | 8 | Saturday |
| 21.1 to 20.2 | Aquarius-Saturn | August | Legs | Nat. Miur | Iron | Blue Sapphire | Blue Sapphire | Violet | 8 | Saturday |
| 21.2 to 20.3 | Pisces-Juptier | Mar-Dec. | Feet | Ferrum Phos. | Tin | Topaj | Topaz | Violet | 3 | Thursday |

# CHAPTER EIGHT

## *Combinations for Excellent Health and Body-Frame*

1. If the lord of the lagna, Jupiter and Venus be placed in the Kendra houses (1, 4, 7, 10) the natives lives happily enjoying all physical and mental comforts for nearly a 100 year.

2. If the 1st house be aspected and occupied by benefics, the native remains healthy throughout his life.

3. If the sign occupying the 1st house be watery, the native will have obese body and if the lord of lagna be well placed aspected by benefic, he will live long. [This combination will be possible only when the ascendants (lagna) be Cancer, Scorpio and Pisces]

4. If the lagna be occupied by a movable sign and aspected by benefics, the native will lead a happy and long life.

5. If the lord of the Moon sign be together with the lord of the lagna, the native will own a robust structure and healthy body.

6. If the owner of the lagna be a natural benefic (like Jupiter, Moon or Mercury) and the lord of the Navamsha Kundali be posited with the lord of the moon sign the native enjoys a long life with a robust frame.

7. If the owner of the lagna be a natural benefic, well placed and aspected by friendly planet, the native enjoys a happy long life free of ailments.

8. If Jupiter, be placed in the 1st house or the 1st house be aspected by Jupiter, the native is endowed with a healthy body.

9. If the lord of the lagna chart and Navamsha chart be placed in watery sign the native gets an obese body.

10. If Jupiter be in 7th and the lagna be having a watery sign, the native gets a fat frame.

11. If the lord of the 2nd house be posited in 1st, 4th, 7th or 10th house with a benefic, the native will have attractive face.

12. If Mars be placed in 7th house from the position of Mercury, the native will be tall and lanky but will have a healthy body with great amount of innate vitality.

13. If the lord of the lagna be placed 5th, 6th, 7th or 8th houses the native will get a powerful frame.

14. If the Sun and Venus be placed in Leo sign and the 10th house be occupied with the Moon in Capricorn, the native will be short-statured. [It is obvious that this shall be applicable to only Aries ascendant].

15. If the moon be placed in 1/2/4/9/10 sign (i.e. in Aries, Taurus, Cancer, Sagittarius and Capricorn) with Aries be the lagna, the native will be a dwarf though of rohust frame.

16. The native will be short statured if the ascendant be Aries, Moon and Sun be placed in the lagna or 12th house and Saturn from the 4th house be aspecting lagna.

17. If Saturn in Aries, Pisces, Capricorn or Scorpio; the Moon associated with malefics : the native will be short statured.

18. If Mars in its own sign be placed with Mercury in 4th house, Saturn be in the lagna, the native will be short statured.

19. If the Moon of Cancer sign be aspected by Saturn and Mars, the native is endowed with a short stature with a hump on the back.

20. If the lagna be occupied by Leo sign with Jupiter also placed in it, Venus be of Cancer sign the Moon of Virgo in 2nd house and the malefics be in 3rd, 6th and 11th house, such a native lives long.

21. Saturn in lagna, Sun and Mars in 12th and the rest of the planets be in 8th the native lives long.

22. The native lives for 86 + years if the lagna be Aries, Sun in Cancer in 4th, Saturn of Pisces in 12th, Mars in 7th and digitally powerful Moon be in 12th house.

23. The Moon in Taurus in 1st house with Mercury, Venus and Jupiter and the rest of the planets in 2nd make the native live for nearly a hundred years.

24. Jupiter of its own sign in the lagna and Venus of Gemini in a Kendra house make the native live for about a hundred years.

25. If barring Rahu as Ketu all the planets be placed in the adjacent Kendra and Trikona houses (like 4, 5 or 9th, 10th) either the child will die soon but if he is made to survive on the strength of a good medical treatment, he may live for a 100 years. [*i.e.*, If such a child survives for about a year, then he will live for 100 years]

26. If 5th and 9th be devoid of any malefic planets, the Kendra houses (1st, 4th, 7th, 10th) devoid of benefics and the 8th be from of evil planet's affliction, the native lives for about a 100 years.

27. If Taurus be the lagna and Venus and Jupiter be placed in Kendra with rest of the planets be in 3rd, 6th, 10th and 11th house, the native lives long.

28. If Cancer be the lagna, Moon be in Taurus, Saturn in Libra, Jupiter in Capricorn, the native leads a happy and contented long life.

29. If Sagittarius be lagna with Venus in the lagna, Jupiter in 7th, Moon in Virgo such a native leads a divine life and lives for a hundred years.

30. If Jupiter be in Pisces, Saturn in 11th, the Sun in 2nd house and Mars in a sign owned by itself, the native lives for a hundred years or so.

31. If Taurus be the sign in 1st house, Jupiter and Mercury in Kendra house and the Moon be of its own sign, the native leads a happy and contented long life.

32. Jupiter in Cancer sign, Mars in 7th, Saturn in 4th with the birth be in day time, the native leads a happy and contented long life.

33. If Jupiter, Saturn and Venus be placed in such a way in the horoscope as to be in the Kendra or Trikona house from each

other (*i.e.* in the 1st, 4th, 7th, 10th or 5th or 9th) the native lives long enjoying all comforts of life.

34. If the 1st house be having Leo sign with all benefics in the Kendra houses and all the malefics be in 3rd, 6th or 11th house, the native lives long.

35. If Cancer be the lagna and all planets be in their exalted or friendly signs (like Jupiter in Cancer, Sun in Leo, Mercury in Virgo etc.) the native like an ancient seer enjoys a long and contented life.

36. If Capricorn be the lagna with the Sun, Mars, Mercury, Venus and Saturn be placed in the lagna, Jupiter be in third house and the native be born during day time, he or she lives long.

37. Jupiter in the Cancer sign in 1st, Saturn in lagna, Sun and Mercury in a stable sign (2nd, 4th, 8th, 11th), Moon in Taurus, Venus in Gemini, the native like ancient sages leads a very long and contented life.

38. If Aries be the lagna, Sun in 10th, Jupiter in Cancer, Mars and Saturn etc. (like strong Malefics in 3rd, 6th or 11th, the native lives for about a hundred years.

39. Cancer lagna with three planets be exalted ensures the native completing the full span (120 years) of human life.

40. Capricorn be the lagna in 15°, Mars in 4th, Moon in the lagna and 7th from Jupiter the native completes the full span of human life (120 years)

41. Jupiter in the lagna (in its own sign, preferably Sagittarius), Moon with Saturn in any house and 10th house be devoid of any evil planet, the native becomes an erudite scholar and completes full life span.

42. Aquarius lagna with Saturn posited in it, and Venus with the Moon in 4th or 9th house, make the native complete full human life span (120 years)

43. Virgo in the lagna, all benefics in the first half (1st to 7th house) with three planets exalted, make the native live for 108 to 120 years.

44. Saturn in the lagna, all malefics in 3rd, 6th or 11th house, Jupiter or Venus in the Kendra house make the native live happily for 120 years.

45. Gemini ascendant, with Mars posited in it, Jupiter in a good house in the second half, exalted Venus and Mercury in Kendra houses make the native live for 108 years.

46. Jupiter and the Moon in Cancer in 1st house, Venus and Mercury in a Kendra house, Sun, Mars and Saturn respectively in 3rd, 6th and 11th house : the native lives for 120 years.

47. Aquarius lagna, Jupiter of Pisces, Venus in 12th of Capricorn, The sun in 1st : the native survives with the help of herbs and roots' potency based treatment for about a 100 years.

48. Libra ascendant and the Sun in 12th in Virgo sign make the native live for more than a hundred years.

49. If the Sun and Mars be together in lagna, Jupiter be in a Kendra house : the native lives for a hundred years.

50. Jupiter in a Kendra (1st, 4th, 7th or 10th) house, Sun and Mars together in 8th : the native lives for about a hundred years. [This combination gives full effect when Jupiter be of Cancer and the lagna be Aries].

51. Leo lagna (ascendant) with the same Navamsha and four benefics he in 1st, 5th or 9th house : the native lives for a 100 years.

52. The Moon in 5th house, Jupiter in 10th with Mars : the native crosses 90 years of age. [This combination is more effective if the ascendant be Aries, Cancer, or Pisces]

53. If the lord of 8th be in own sign or Saturn be in 8th house, despite leading a sickly life the native lives long.

54. If the lords of the lagna, 8th or 10th he in a Kendra of Trikona (5th or 9th) house or in the 11th the native lives for 96 years.

55. If Saturn be in the sign owned by itself, in its exalted sign or in 3rd, 6th, 10th or 11th house, or if Saturn, as the 8th lord he posited in 5th house the native lives for 96 years. [This yoga shows its best effect for Taurus, Gemini, Leo, Sagittarius or Capricorn ascendants.

56. If the lords of the 8th or 1st house be posited in 8th or 11th house the native lives for 96 years.

57. If either of the lords of the lagna, 8th or 10th be posited together with Saturn in a Kendra (1st, 4th, 7th or 10th) house, the native lives for 96 years.

58. If the 10th lord be in its exalted sign and posited in the 5th house or the lord of the 8th be in a Kendra along with the benefics, the native lives for 96 years. [This shows its best effect for the natives of the Pisces ascendants]

59. Malefics be placed in 3rd, 6th or 11th house and benefics is a Kendra or Trikona house the native lives long.

60. Benefics in 6, 7, 8 and malefics in 3, 6, 11 (houses) make the native live for 90 plus age.

61. If the lord of the 8th be in 1st with Jupiter or Venus aspecting it, the native will live for 90 years.

62. If all the planets be placed in 3rd, 4th and 8th houses, the native lives for 96 years of age.

63. If either the lords of the 6th 12th be in the 1st house or the 10th lord be in a Kendra house of the lord of the lagna be in a Kendra or Trikona house, the native lives for 90 plus years.

64. A very strong lagna lord, the placement of all benefics in a Kendra house make the native live for 96 years of age.

65. If the lagna lord be powerfully placed in a Kendra house bearing the aspect of the benefics but unaspected by evil planets : the native enjoys kingly comforts and lives for 96 years.

66. If an odd sign (1, 3, 5, 7, 9, 11) be in the lagna and all planets be in the odd signs, the native gets full favour from luck and lives healthily for 90 years.

67. If all the four Kendra houses (1st, 4th, 7th, 10th) be occupied by benefics, no planet in the 8th and the Moon be placed in the 6th house the native lives for 86 years.

68. If Taurus be in 1st house, the lord of the lagna Venus be aspecting the lagna and all benefics be in the Kendra houses: the native lives healthily for 85 years.

69. The same is the consequence (as given is above) if the lagna be Sagittarius with its lord Jupiter be casting a direct aspect on the 1st house.

70. Jupiter in the lagna, also in its own sign in the Navamsha Chart and the Sun and Saturn be in the Kendra houses : the native lives for 90 plus years.

71. If the sign in the lagna be either Taurus, Leo, Virgo, Capricorn or Aquarius with Mars either in Aries or Scorpio (its own) sign and Mercury and Venus be conjunct either in a kendra or Trikona house, the native will live happily for 85 years.

72. Virgo be the ascendant with its lord Mercury aspecting it while all benefics in the Kendra houses : the native lives for 84 years.

73. If the benefics be in the first six houses and malefics in the remaining six houses : the native is a virtuous being, leads a noble life and lives for 80 years.

74. If Jupiter aspects powerfully placed Moon in any lagna, the native will live for 80 years.

75. Cancer be the lagna with the lord of the lagna Moon be powerful and aspected by Jupiter : the native will live for 80 years.

76. If Jupiter be exalted, placed in the Kendra or Trikona house and the lord of the lagna be also powerful : 80 year's life span.

77. If the lord of the lagna be strong, powerful Mercury in the Kendra or Trikona house and Jupiter be powerfully placed in a good house : 80 year's life span.

78. Benefics in the Kendra houses, Aries be the lagna with Mars (the lord of the lagna) aspecting the lagna make the native live for 75 years.

79. If the lord of the lagna, well-placed and aspecting the lagna, with all benefics in good houses : 75 years life span.

80. Powerful Saturn aspecting 1st house having Capricorn sign with benefics in the Kendra or Trikona house : seventy plus will be native's life span.

81. Mars in the 5th house, the Sun in the 7th and Saturn in Aries : the native will healthy live for 70 plus years.

82. If Saturn of Aries be in a Kendra or Trikona house, the Sun and Mercury be also in a Kendra house with benefics : the native will be a noble person, well-versed in Dharma and live in the prime of health for 70 plus years.

83. Benefics in the Kendra houses; 8th house be unoccupied by any benefic and the lord of the lagna be aspected by benefics : the native will earn his or her wherewithal through immoral means but will live healthily for 70 plus years.

84. No matter what sign be in the 1st house, if the Sun be occupying it in association either with Saturn or Mars, Jupiter be weak and the Moon be either in 12th or 5th, the native will live with good health for 70 plus years.

85. If the 10th house from the lagna be occupied by Mercury, Venus, Moon or Jupiter in conjunction, the native will live for 70 years.

86. If the Moon and the Sun be in 10th, Saturn in the lagna, Jupiter in 4th : the native will own large estate and enjoying highly comforts shall live upto 68 years. [This yoga fructifies better in Aries, Virgo and Sagittarius ascendants]

87. If Jupiter be in the lagna, Sun, Saturn and Venus be conjunct in any house and the benefics be aspecting lagna, the native will live for 68 years.

88. If Jupiter, Mercury and the Sun be in the lagna, Saturn be in Pisces sign and the moon be in 12th house, the native living in luxury will enjoy kingly comforts and shall live for 66 years. [This yoga shows better results for Cancer and Jupiter ascendants].

89. If Cancer be the ascendant with the Moon placed in it, Saturn be in Aries (debilited), Sun is 7th : the native will be a foremost scholar but will live for 65 years.

90. If the malefics be a 3rd, 4th, 2nd, 5th, 8th and 11th house, the native lives for 64 years.

91. A weak lagna lord placement of Jupiter in a Kendra or Trikona house and existence of malefics in 8th make the native live for 64 years.

92. If any malefic like Saturn be placed in 6th or 8th house : the native lives for 64 years which is held to be middle age by the astrological norms.

93. If the malefics and the benefics be placed together in the Kendra and Trikona houses the native will live for 64 years.

94. Birth in the day time with the existence of cruel planets (like Saturn, Mars, Sun or Rahu, Ketu) makes the native live for 64 years.

95. If Jupiter be placed in the sign owned by its natural enemy and in the 3rd, 9th or 5th house, the native lives for 58 years.

96. Jupiter in Cancer placed in the 9th house with the Moon aspecting it makes the native live for more than 90 years.

97. The Moon placed in Taurus and aspected by Jupiter makes the native live for 70 years.

98. If Jupiter in Cancer be placed in any Kendra houses (preferably 1st or 10th) the native lives for the full span of human life.

99. If Mars and the Moon be together in Lagna aspected by Jupiter make the native life for 80 years.

# CHAPTER NINE

# Birth-Month-wise Disease Proneness

1. If you are born between 20th February and 21st March you are likely to have good health in general but after 23rd year you may start falling sick. The years of your life viz 28th, 40th, 42nd, 48th, 50th, 54th, 58th and 60th would be bad from the health point of view. Among the sicknesses that are likely to trouble you, the prominent ones are : gout, clotting of the blood, skin-related diseases and other endemic diseases. In the years mentioned above these will show their pronounced effect. You are likely to live for 71 years.

2. If you are born between 21st March and 20th April you are likely to have the effect of Mars on your personality. Your body frame would be sparsely built but you will have broad shoulders. Doing much of physical labour will be harmful for you. Before the onset of any ailment the invariable symptom will be headache. You will have constipative tendency. Wearing Coral (Moonga) will be helpful. Normally you will have good health but likely to be troubled by blood-pressure fluctuation. For the persons born in this month sleeping for at least 7 hours in a day is a 'must'. You will be susceptible to cold. You are prone to suffer minor accidents but they won't prove much damaging. November, January and April months are to be especially watched from health point of view. You are prone to suffering heat strokes. Hence in summer you have to be extra careful. Be wary about the water-borne diseases in the dark fortnights (Krishna Daksha) of the above mentioned months. You may live upto 75 years.

3. If you are born between 21st April and 20th May, you will have a weak or suceptible throat and heart. So you have to be extra careful about the ailments related to these two organs. You are advised to eat easily digestible food and stay away from cold drinks and frozen edibles. Onset of any trouble will afflict your throat region. The years you will be prone to becoming ill or getting involved in any accident are 6th, 8th, 10th, 16th, 21st, 25th, 30th, 46th, 52nd and 55th. You are likely to survive till 85th year of your age. You will have a slightly obese body.

4. If you are born between 21st May to 20th June, you will have lean and thin body frame. You will have powerful eyes which may be dark or dark blue. You are susceptible to heart ailments. Spicy food and liquor are not good for your health. A little of physical exercise will prove good to you to keep healthy. You are likely to suffer sickness in 1st, 4th, 9th, 11th, 16th, 20th, 26th, 28th, 32nd, 44th, 45th, 56th, 66th and 71st years. Natives born in this period must assiduously avoid foul company. You may live for 75 years.

5. If you are born between 21st June and 20th July, you will have a weak digestive system. Any excesses committed in having food neither at the regular hours or in the fixed quantity will give rise to various ailments related to digestive malfunctioning. Since you are over-cautious about your health, your brooding nature will further aggravate the ailments you suffer. Dyspepsia and diarrhoea may repeated by afflict you. Natives of this period may have frequent bouts of ailments. Upto first 10 years of your life you might have faced various worries about your health. The years to be further watched from the health point of view are 14th, 16th, 17th, 23rd, 26th, 30th, 35th, 38th, 45th, 47th, 49th, 56th, 62nd, 64th, 68th and you may live upto 70 years. Waning moon may invariably create trouble for you from the health's point of view.

6. If you are born between 21st July and 20th August, normally you will enjoy fairly good health but may get afflicted with heart related ailments whose fount will be in the

malfunctioning of the respiratory system. You are advised to take adequate rest every day particularly after a heavy toil in order to avoid undue pressure on the heart. Edibles which produce heat in the body should not form your stable diet. Eating clean and easily digestible food is ideal for you. In the initial years you may suffer frequent attacks of sickness. The problem of blood pressure will start afflicting you around 42 years of age. Be careful about it since it may even cause paralysis. You may live upto 75 years. Avoid drastic changes in your life style.

7. If you are born between 21st August and 20th September, though you will be endowed with a robust system, blood pressure related ailments and nervous disorders are likely to trouble you. Taking long walks in a clean and pore atmosphere and sustenance on simple and easily digestible food will keep you in good trim. Particularly after 45 years you have to be especially careful about your health. Since you are of brooding type, your physical trouble may get aggravated by your powerful imagination. If you take the necessary precautions, stay away from narcotic and analgesic drugs you may live upto 85 years.

8. If you are born between 21 September and 20th October, normally your health will be good but you have to be careful about cold-induced afflictions. Visit to, and stay at hilly stations or places where oxygen may be rarefied is not advisable for you. You have been endowed with a weak bronchia tract and hence you should be guarded about letting your body suffer drastic temperature variations. Those born in this period should also be extra careful about the various epidemics like cholera, plague etc. Between 14 and 24 and 44 and 66 years you have to stay doubly vigilant to ensure your good health. Avoid dust and grime since they may trigger allergic reactions in your body. You may live upto 84 years but the period between 64 to 84 years would warrant greater attention.

9. If your are born between 21st October to 20th November you are a person who very rarely lose your equanimity. In order

to keep yourself free of ailments you must drink a lot of cool water or eat those edibles that produce cool effect in your system. Persons born in this period rarely die an untimely death. Even though you may be afflicted with ailments, no drastic (allopathic) treatment would be able to cure you. The disease from years are 3rd, 8th, 10th, 12th, 20th, 25th, 29th, 42nd, 45th, 48th, 65th, 74th, 79th and 80th. You may live for 85 years. Particularly the bright fortnight of every month of the aforesaid year would cause more physical troubles. You must avoid those edibles that produce wind in the system.

10. If you are born between 21 November and 20th December, you will, in general, keep good health. Weakest part of your system is lungs. So you will have to be careful about respiratory disorders. Your staying in the sun will keep you particularly healthy. Health-wise initial years upto 10 year would be rather bad and then 58 to 64 years period. Keeping a schedule of going for a leisurely walk every day will keep you in good trim. You may live upto 85 years.

11. If you are born between 21st December to 20th January, your weak organs would be kidney and those that are involved in digestive process. You are susceptible to cold and your body will have a tendency to become numb rather unusually. Pneumonia and bronchitis are the ailments that might frequently afflict you. Between 18 and 25 years you may have the afflictions that produce eruptions on the face and body like small pox. You should also be vary of the such eruptions as caused by the insect-bite. Your body would be allergic to having any type of poison inflicting it. Any fall or accident in which blood may trickle out should be carefully attended to, else it might develop into a big headache. The persons born in this period may live upto 80 years.

12. If you are born between 21st January to 20 February, your congenitally weak organ of the body may be the eyes. Apart from them your skin may also be extremely sensitive. So you have to be careful about the texture of the clothes you wear. It is better not to wear synthetic clothes. Diabetes may also afflict you at advanced age since your body may be generally

deficient to absorb nutrients from the food you intake Blood Pressure and piles may also trouble you at advanced age. So you must not maintain a sedentary life style. Taking a long walks, particularly early in the morning may keep you away from these problems. If all goes well you may live upto 90 years.

## Bad Years for Those Born On :

1. **Sunday**      : 17th, 26th, 35th, 44th, 53rd, 62nd years
2. **Monday**      : 39th, 52nd, 55th, 63rd, and 68th
3. **Tuesday**     : 26th, 27th, 31st, 34th
4. **Wednesday**   : 19th, 21st, 25th, 27th, 34th, 38th, 53rd
5. **Thursday**    : 14th, 18th, 27th, 23rd, 29th, 43rd, 49th, 62nd, 68th
6. **Friday**      : 12th, 21st, 29th, 43rd, 48th, 53rd, 55th, 59th, 65th
7. **Saturday**    : 28th, 42nd, 49th, 52nd, 57th, 65th, 68th, 71st.

# CHAPTER TEN

# Ailments, Glands and Planets : Ready Reckoner Chart

1. **Appendicitis** : Afflicted Moon and the 6th house are to be noted. Mars with a Node (Rahu and Ketu) is also responsible.
2. **Hair Problem** : Involve Mars, Mercury and Saturn.
3. **Right hand** : Rahu and 3rd house.
4. **Left hand** : Mars and 11th house.
5. **Waist** : It is governed by Rahu.
6. **Spleen** : Apart from Jupiter, Saturn is also involved.
7. **Right Thigh** : Venus.
8. **Right Foot** : Saturn.
9. **Liver** : Jupiter.
10. **Left Thigh** : Moon.
11. **Left Foot** : Saturn.
12. **Intestines** : Jupiter and Ketu.
13. **Stomach** : Jupiter and Rahu.
14. **Head** : Afflicted Sun and Mars.
15. **Brain** : Sun And Mercury.
16. **Neck** : Mars, Rahu and the 3rd house.
17. **Bones** : Sun, Mars, Rahu, Saturn.
18. **Arthritis** : Saturn and the houses 1, 6, 8, 12.
19. **Heart** : 4th and 5th house, Sun, Mars and Mercury in the 4th or 5th.
20. **Lungs and Chest** : Moon and the 4th house.
21. **Kidney** : Venus, Libra, and the 7th house.

22. **Liver** : Sun, Jupiter, 5th house and Leo.

23. **Ear** : Gemini and Virgo, Mercury, Mars and Rahu in the 3rd, lord of 2nd in 1st or 8th.

24. **Right Ear** : Afflictions related to this part refer to Jupiter and the 3rd house.

25. **Left Ear** : Related affliction refer to Mars and 11th house.

26. **Tongue** : Rahu, Saturn and the houses 6th, 8th and 12th.

27. **Eye** : Sun, Venus, houses 2 and 12 are important. Moon, Mars, Saturn and Rahu are to be examined. Right eye involves the Sun and 2nd house. Left eye refers to the Moon and 12th house.

28. **Nose** : Saturn and the Moon, houses 6, 8, 12.

29. **Teeth** : Rahu and Saturn in 2nd, associated with the lord of Lagna. Mercury and Saturn are also to be examined.

30. **Skin** : Saturn is the chief indicator along with Mars, houses 1, 6, 8 are also to be considered.

31. **Leucoderma** : Refers to Venus; consider also Rahu.

32. **Diabetes** : Jupiter, Venus and the Sun.

33. **Generative Organs** : Mars, Venus and Rahu.

34. **Urinary Disorders** : Refer mainly to Moon and Mars.

35. **Hydrocele** : Mars, Saturn, Rahu in Lagna. Lord of the 1st in 8th with Rahu; Jupiter and Rahu in lagna.

36. **Leprosy** : Houses 1 and 6 are involved. The luminaries (the Moon and the Sun) Mars, Saturn, Mercury and the Nodes (Rahu or Ketu) are to be considered. Prime indicators, however, are Mars and Rahu. Ketu and Mars combination also gives rise to this trouble.

37. **Tuberculosis** : Houses 1, 6 and 8, Mercury with Mars in 6th aspected by the Moon and Venus. Saturn, however, is the chief indicator. Mars and the Nodes (Rahu and Ketu) are also to be considered.

38. **Paralysis** : Saturn with Jupiter in Gemini, Libra or Aquarius in the 6th; The Moon and the Mercury afflicted by Saturn and Rahu; the Sun in lagna afflicted by Mars and Saturn in

Leo or in houses owned by Mars, Mercury or Saturn; Moon and Mercury afflicted by Saturn and Rahu.

39. **Mental Affliction** : Insanity is the dominant one. The houses involved are 3, 5 and 9; sometimes 7th also some combinations include Jupiter in the 1st and Mars in the 7th; Saturn in the 1st, and Mars in 5th, 7th or 9th; the Moon, Mars and Mercury in one Kendra house; conjunctions of the Moon and Ketu; Mars and Mercury in the 6th or 8th.

## Glands

The planets governing the glands are the following :

1. **Sun** : Thyroid and front Pituitary
2. **Moon** : Thyroid
3. **Moon and Mars** : Back Pituitary
4. **Mars and Ketu** : Pineal.
5. **Mars and Saturn** : Parathyroid
6. **Mars and Jupiter** : Thyroid
7. **Mars, Jupiter and Venus** : Pancreas
8. **Mars and Venus** : Adrenalin and sex glands
9. **Mars** : Adrenalin, Gonad
10. **Mercury** : Back Pituitary, Parathyroid
11. **Venus** : Pancreas
12. **Saturn** : Pituitary Adrenalin.

As is apparent the areas of control of different planets over afflictions frequently overlap because human body is a single organic whole. As such it is unavoidable. However, what is suggested through this ready reckoner chart is the areas or the planets that are to be concentrated on to detect the cause of various ailments. Moreover it depends upon the astro-medical practitioner to identify the causes by his or her experience.

# CHAPTER ELEVEN

# *End of Life*

Although many readers would find this chapter rather incongruous in the book of this kind, yet the basic fact can't be denied that death is a certainty and astrology can suggest some indications to tell which way death may approach the native. In order to complete this book in every way, it was thought wise to add this chapter also.

As has been suggested earlier, astrology has identified the 'Maraka' planets also. Normally the lord of 2nd and 7th is called a 'Maraka' which literally means killer but in the astrological context it means the planet which may induce the conditions as much adverse as to cause the native's death. We are giving below the lagna-wise planets which are malefic, benefic, friendly or 'maraka' to the native of a particular lagna. [Yoga-Karaka are the planets especially good to the nature of a particular ascendant.]

The eighth house should be judged to find out the possible way of the native meeting his or her end. The other factors of consideration are the planets tenanting the eighth house, aspects received by the eighth house, and the navamsha tenanted by the lord of the eight house.

Various planets may cause death in different ways. Their influences in bringing the life of a man to an end are as follows :

1. **Sun** : Fever, Stomach, ailments, lethal weapon, accidents — Particularly caused by fire.

2. **Moon** : Bodily disorders caused by excessive accumulation of water in the body organs, small pox, tuberculosis.

3. **Mars** : Black magic, murder, fire, blood oozing including haemorrhage.

4. **Mercury** : Delirium, insanity, meningitis, anaemia.

5. **Jupiter** : Sudden death by heart attack.

6. **Venus** : Sexual diseases.

7. **Saturn** : Typhoid, worms, gastric trouble, ulcer.

8. **Rahu** : Small pox, poison, leprosy or other incurable diseases.

9. **Ketu** : Accidents connected with water, suicide.

When the lord of the eighth house, or the eighth house itself occupies the various signs, death will be caused by different kind of maladies. They can be listed as follows.

1. **Aries** : Fever, indigestion, gastric troubles.

2. **Taurus** : Inflammation of the lungs, throat troubles.

3. **Gemini** : Stomach ulcers, diseases connected with the lungs, kidney failures.

4. **Cancer** : Meningitis, Gastric troubles, liver/spleen/kidney disorders

5. **Leo** : Dog bite or other animal bite, fever, boils, drugs, attack by enemies.

6. **Virgo** : Diseases connected with sex, fall from height.

7. **Libra** : Fever, typhoid, malaria, meningitis or other diseases of the brain.

8. **Scorpio** : Dysentry, Anaemia, diphtheria, liver and kidney related ailments.

9. **Sagittarius** : Lethal weapons, accidents connected with water, fall from height.

10. **Capricorn** : Diseases connected with the brain, Motor Neuron Disease.

11. **Aquarius** : Ailments of the heart, consumption, fever, asthma, delirium.

12. **Pisces** : Elephantiasis, too much of water accumulation in the body, dropsy, accidents in water.

The affect of the adverse planets major period may accumulate these possibilities if the planets in transit are also bad. Hence for determining any particular period both the Dashas (the Dashas from natal chart and of transit) should be considered.

# The Chart indicating Mutual Relationship Among the Planets

| Lagna | Malefic | Benefic | Yoga-Karak | Maraka |
|-------|---------|---------|------------|--------|
| Aries | Saturn, Mercury Venus | Jupiter, Sun | | Saturn, Mercury, Venus |
| Taurus | Jupiter, Venus, Moon | Saturn, Sun | Saturn | Jupiter, Venus, Moon |
| Gemini | Mars, Jupiter, Sun | Venus | | Mars, Jupiter Saturn |
| Cancer | Venus, Mercury | Mars, Jupiter | Mars | Sun, Venus, Mercury |
| Leo | Mercury, Venus | Mars | | Mercury, Venus |
| Virgo | Mars, Jupiter, Moon | Venus | Venus, Mercury | Jupiter, Sun |
| Libra | Jupiter, Sun, Mars | Saturn, Mercury | Saturn | Jupiter, Sun |
| Scorpio | Mercury, Mars, Venus | Moon | Sun, Moon | Mercury, Mars, Venus |
| Sagittarius | Venus | Mars, Sun | Sun, Mercury | Saturn, Venus |
| Capricorn | Mars, Jupiter Moon | Venus, Mercury | Venus | Mars, Jupiter, Moon |
| Aquarius | Jupiter, Moon, Mars | Venus | Mars | Moon, Mars |
| Pisces | Saturn, Venus, Sun, Mercury | Mars, Moon | Mars, Jupiter | Saturn, Venus, Sun, Mercury |

# CHAPTER TWELVE

# The Dasha System

Dasha literally means the state or the condition one is in but in astrological parlance it shows the period in which one planet's influence dominates. In this system, as hinted before there are two kinds of 'Dashas" : the 'Gochar (Transit) Dasha' and the 'Natal Dasha'. In fact the natal chart shows the position of the planets vis-a-vis the sign rising at the horizon at the time of one's birth. It is believed that exactly at the time a life comes into an existence in worldly sense, the planet; radiation have their greatest effect. The natal chart shows that effect's photostat copy *i.e.* the position of the planets and their effect on the human body as they greet it. But the planets, continue to move after that since they are not static. So the subsequent effect of the planet's position on the person is determined taking the moon sign as the basic reckoning point. Suppose the native's moon sign is Taurus, the lagna is Libra, and the Nakshatra is Rohini. Going by the degrees the Moon is in Taurus in Rohini it is determined which planet would show its maximum effect first. That is called the Dasha of the planet. It is further divided into the minor or such minor period of the planets showing their effect in a well determined order. The cycle of the Dasha starts the following way : Sun, Moon, Mars, Rahu, Jupiter, Saturn, Mercury, Ketu and Venus. In case your Dasha starts from the Moon, it would be followed by Mars, Rahu and so or till you reach the last planet before the Moon, that is the Sun. So the natal Dasha is calculated in this manner. If you have your Dasha beginning from the Moon, and the sub period would also be that of the moon as also the minor sub period. The Dasha system divides a man's life into periods such as major period and minor sub-periods, which are characterised by the various planets coming in the regular cycles. Moon is the starting point in life. It is believed by the seers of Hindu Astrology that the Moon exercised the greatest influence over man's life.

In India the two type of the Dasha systems in vogue : the VIMSHOTTARI SYSTEM and the ASHTTOTARI SYSTEM. But we are basing our calculation on the VIMSHOTTARI SYSTEM which is believed to be more popular and held to be more accurate. This system, Vimshottari believes that the human life span is of 120 years. Each planet has its marked period of influences as follows :

| | |
|---|---|
| Sun's period | 6 years |
| Moon's period | 10 years |
| Mar's period | 7 years |
| Rahu's period | 18 years |
| Jupiter's period | 16 years |
| Saturn's period | 19 years |
| Mercury's period | 17 years |
| Ketu's period | 7 years |
| Venus's period | 20 years |
| Total | 120 years |

They are the major periods for which the planets exercise their maximum influences in a fixed order as explained above.

So, for calculating the Dashas what one needs is the 'Nakshatras at the time of the native's birth position 'Nakshatras' are actually zodiacal divisions in angular distance of 13°20′ each and they are a convenient order of calculating the longitude of the planets. Each Nakshatra is named after a lord, and a fixed point. For example Mesha coincides with 'Krittika' Nakshatras. [Their order has been explained in the first chapter].

The Major period of any planet is, as explained, determined by finding which part of the Nakshatras has been covered by the Moon. Suppose three parts of the Nakshatra has been covered. Now, there are four division in all and we know that the Moon Dasha lasts for 10 years [Four parts = 10 years, then one part = 2.5 years]. Hence the period of the Moon Dasha one has to pass through is 2-5 years. [This part is not being elaborated since now-a-days we get computer-made horoscope having precisely marked Dasha of each planet.]

The effect of the Dasha by natal chart depends upon the position of the planet in the natal chart. If the planet is well placed, aspected and occupying favourable sign, it would be good. In the horoscope given as example in the second chapter, concentrate on Saturn. It is posited in 9th in the company of its friends Rahu and Venus, in the sign Gemini. Since it is Yogakaraka for the Libra lagna, being the lord of a Kendra and Trikona house, its major period or even minor or sub minor period will be good and favourable to the native. This way for every planet the Dasha, Antara dasha or Pratyanter Dasha effects can be analysed.

The general impact of the Dasha of the nine planets as the lord of the twelve houses can be studied in the following way.

*Lord of the First House* : The native will be surrounded by relatives and well wishers.

*Lord of the Second House* : The native will be setting up a family, and home life will be a happy one.

*Lord of the Third House* : Results are unfavourable. Failures and disappointments.

*Lord of the Fourth House* : Acquisition of properties and other assets.

*Lord of the Fifth House* : Child birth

*Lord of the Sixth House* : Danger from enemies

*Lord of the Seventh House* : Marriage

*Lord of the Eighth House* : Recovery from illness

*Lord of the Ninth House* : Profit in various undertakings

*Lord of the Tenth House* : Good luck in speculation

*Lord of the Eleventh House* : Gains in various enterprises

*Lord of the Twelfth House* : Illness, expenditure, mental worries.

These effects magnify when the lords are strong. During the major Dasha of a planet, its own sub-period will be of not much significance.

During the periods of "Yoga Karakas", as hinted before the malefics are incapable of effecting their evil influence. And, of course, during the major Dasha of a malefic planet the sub-period of a good planet, which is not influenced by the ruling planet, is incapable of effecting good results. However, those that are influenced effect mixed results.

The highly benign effects of a planet that produces Raja Yoga, show themselves in the sub-period of the "Maraka"—Killing-planet, during the major Dasha of the former. And the benevolent effects go on increasing in the sub-periods of malefic planets during the same major period.

The major Dashas of those planets that are the lords of the third, fifth or the seventh Nakshatras, counted from the birth star, are also malefic.

Generally speaking, the favourable planets begin to give out their good effects when the Sun or Jupiter brings in their sub-periods in the major Dasha of the former.

The various influences that will prevail during the periods of rule of the different planets may be set out as follows :

Sun    : When he is strong, in his major period or minor period, is capable of bestowing upon the native wealth, fame, happiness, well being of family, betterment of general living conditions, conquest of enemies, and other benefits.

When he is adverse, by his position or aspect, the results will be sickness in the family, sorrow, danger to the life of father and mother, extravagence, fear from enemies, disappointments in job and other misfortunes.

Moon    : In his good aspect he bestows upon the native prosperity, health, well being of father and mother, increase in assets, happiness in family life, success in intellectual pursuits and other blessings.

In his adverse aspect however, he brings sorrow, ill-health to mother and father, loss of money, loss of assets, ill-health and even death.

Mars    : In his favourable aspect Mars confers upon his native, during his rulership, riches, clothes and ornaments, profits in business, fulfilment of desires, and general happiness.

In his adverse aspect however he turns the native into a man of loose morals, a chief, blackmailer, and one who is disliked by everybody.

Mercury : During the rulership of Mercury, in his good aspect, he confers upon the native a sharp intellect and scholarship. The native will pursue literary activities and receive acclaim.

Mercury in his unfavourable aspect can cause the native to become dull and thick headed.

Jupiter : In his beneficial aspect he confers upon the native the highest honours and a most glorious life.

In his adverse aspect he can be very evil. He causes loss of money and friends, disgrace in society, ill-health to members of the family and other misfortunes.

Venus : In his favourable aspect he bestows upon the native great artistic achievements, happy marital relations, birth of son, gains in business and high social recognition.

When adverse, he can bring upon the native ill-health, expenses and other displeasures.

Saturn : During his rulership, in his benevolent aspect, he offers the native various gains, leadership in society, excellent health and strength and a scholarship of occult studies.

But in his adverse aspect he can bring upon the native untold misery. The native will suffer notoriety, bondage, imprisonment, debts, madness, slander, poverty and all kinds of other misfortunes.

Rahu : In his good aspect he can confer upon the native, during his rulership, marriage, birth of a son, wealth, expansion of landed properties, devotion to God, and other benefits.

An adverse Rahu will mean, ill-health in family, disappointments in the various pursuits, loss of health and even death due to poisoning.

Ketu : During his rulership, in his favourable aspect, he can confer upon the native riches, power, domestic happiness and other benefits.

A bad Ketu will mean frustrations and failures, death of close friends, loss of assets by theft, and other unforeseen troubles.

# The Tables showing Major, Minor and Sub-minor Periods

## SUN'S PERIODS

| | | | | Sub-Periods | | | | | |
|---|---|---|---|---|---|---|---|---|---|
| | Sun | Moon | Mars | Rahu | Juptier | Saturn | Mercury | Ketu | Venus | Total |
| Years | 0 | 0 | 0 | 0 | 0 | 0 | 0 | 0 | 1 | 6 |
| Months | 3 | 6 | 4 | 10 | 9 | 11 | 10 | 4 | 0 | 0 |
| Days | 18 | 0 | 6 | 24 | 18 | 12 | 6 | 6 | 0 | 0 |

## Minor Sub-periods

### 1. M.S.P. of Sun

| | M | D | H |
|---|---|---|---|
| Sun | 0 | 5 | 9.6 |
| Moon | 0 | 9 | 0.0 |
| Mars | 0 | 6 | 7.2 |
| Rahu | 0 | 16 | 4.8 |
| Jupiter | 0 | 14 | 9.6 |
| Saturn | 0 | 17 | 2.4 |
| Mercury | 0 | 15 | 7.2 |
| Ketu | 0 | 6 | 7.2 |
| Venus | 0 | 18 | 0.0 |
| Total | 3 | 18 | 0.0 |

### 2. M.S.P. of Moon

| | M | D | H |
|---|---|---|---|
| Moon | 0 | 15 | 0 |
| Mars | 0 | 10 | 12 |
| Rahu | 0 | 27 | 0 |
| Jupiter | 0 | 24 | 0 |
| Saturn | 0 | 28 | 12 |
| Mercury | 0 | 25 | 12 |
| Ketu | 0 | 10 | 12 |
| Venus | 1 | 0 | 0 |
| Sun | 0 | 9 | 0 |
| Total | 6 | 0 | 0 |

### 3. M.S.P. of Mars

| | M | D | H |
|---|---|---|---|
| Mars | 0 | 7 | 8.4 |
| Rahu | 0 | 18 | 21.6 |
| Jupiter | 0 | 16 | 19.2 |
| Saturn | 0 | 19 | 22.8 |
| Mercury | 0 | 17 | 20.4 |
| Ketu | 0 | 7 | 8.4 |
| Venus | 0 | 21 | 0.0 |
| Sun | 0 | 6 | 7.2 |
| Moon | 0 | 10 | 12.0 |
| Total | 4 | 6 | 0.0 |

## 4. M.S.P. of Rahu

| | M | D | H |
|---|---|---|---|
| Rahu | 1 | 18 | 14.4 |
| Jupiter | 1 | 13 | 4.8 |
| Saturn | 1 | 21 | 7.2 |
| Mercury | 1 | 15 | 21.6 |
| Ketu | 0 | 18 | 21.6 |
| Venus | 1 | 24 | 0.0 |
| Sun | 0 | 16 | 4.8 |
| Moon | 0 | 27 | 0.0 |
| Mars | 0 | 18 | 21.6 |
| **Total** | **10** | **6** | **0.0** |

## 5. M.S.P. of Jupiter

| | M | D | H |
|---|---|---|---|
| Jupiter | 1 | 8 | 9.6 |
| Saturn | 1 | 15 | 14.4 |
| Mercury | 1 | 10 | 19.2 |
| Ketu | 0 | 16 | 19.2 |
| Venus | 1 | 18 | 0.0 |
| Sun | 0 | 14 | 9.6 |
| Moon | 0 | 24 | 0.0 |
| Mars | 0 | 16 | 19.2 |
| Rahu | 1 | 13 | 4.8 |
| **Total** | **9** | **18** | **0.0** |

## 6. M.S.P. of Saturn

| | M | D | H |
|---|---|---|---|
| Saturn | 1 | 24 | 3.6 |
| Mercury | 1 | 18 | 10.8 |
| Ketu | 0 | 19 | 22.8 |
| Venus | 1 | 27 | 0.0 |
| Sun | 0 | 17 | 0.4 |
| Moon | 0 | 28 | 12.0 |
| Mars | 0 | 19 | 22.8 |
| Rahu | 1 | 21 | 7.2 |
| Jupiter | 1 | 15 | 14.6 |
| **Total** | **11** | **12** | **0.0** |

## 7. M.S.P. of Mercury

| | M | D | H |
|---|---|---|---|
| Mercury | 1 | 13 | 8.4 |
| Ketu | 0 | 17 | 20.4 |
| Venus | 1 | 21 | 0.0 |
| Sun | 0 | 15 | 7.2 |
| Moon | 0 | 25 | 12.0 |
| Mars | 0 | 17 | 20.4 |
| Rahu | 1 | 15 | 21.6 |
| Jupiter | 1 | 10 | 19.2 |
| Saturn | 1 | 18 | 10.8 |
| **Total** | **10** | **6** | **0.0** |

## 8. M.S.P. of Ketu

| | M | D | H |
|---|---|---|---|
| Ketu | 0 | 7 | 8.4 |
| Venus | 0 | 21 | 0.0 |
| Sun | 2 | 6 | 7.2 |
| Moon | 0 | 10 | 12.0 |
| Mars | 0 | 7 | 8.4 |
| Rahu | 0 | 18 | 21.6 |
| Jupiter | 0 | 16 | 19.6 |
| Saturn | 0 | 19 | 22.8 |
| Mercury | 0 | 17 | 20.4 |
| **Total** | **4** | **6** | **0.0** |

## 9. M.S.P. of Venus

| | M | D | H |
|---|---|---|---|
| Venus | 2 | 0 | 0 |
| Sun | 0 | 18 | 0 |
| Moon | 1 | 0 | 0 |
| Mars | 0 | 21 | 0 |
| Rahu | 1 | 24 | 0 |
| Jupiter | 1 | 18 | 0 |
| Saturn | 1 | 27 | 0 |
| Mercury | -1 | 21 | 0 |
| Ketu | 0 | 21 | 0 |
| **Total** | **12** | **0** | **0** |

## MOON'S PERIODS

### Sub-Periods

| | Moon | Mars | Rahu | Juptier | Saturn | Mercury | Ketu | Venus | Sun | Total |
|---|---|---|---|---|---|---|---|---|---|---|
| Years | 0 | 0 | 1 | 1 | 1 | 1 | 0 | 0 | 1 | 10 |
| Months | 10 | 7 | 6 | 4 | 7 | 5 | 7 | 8 | 6 | 0 |
| Days | 0 | 0 | 0 | 0 | 0 | 0 | 0 | 0 | 0 | 0 |

### Minor Sub-periods

#### 1. M.S.P. of Moon

| | M | D | H |
|---|---|---|---|
| Moon | 0 | 25 | 0 |
| Mars | 0 | 17 | 12 |
| Rahu | 1 | 15 | 0 |
| Jupiter | 1 | 10 | 0 |
| Saturn | 1 | 17 | 12 |
| Mercury | 1 | 12 | 12 |
| Ketu | 0 | 17 | 12 |
| Venus | 1 | 20 | 0 |
| Sun | 0 | 15 | 0 |
| Total | 10 | 0 | 0 |

#### 2. M.S.P. of Mars

| | M | D | H |
|---|---|---|---|
| Mars | 0 | 12 | 6 |
| Rahu | 1 | 1 | 12 |
| Jupiter | 0 | 28 | 0 |
| Saturn | 1 | 3 | 6 |
| Mercury | 0 | 29 | 18 |
| Ketu | 0 | 12 | 6 |
| Venus | 1 | 5 | 0 |
| Sun | 0 | 10 | 12 |
| Moon | 0 | 17 | 12 |
| Total | 7 | 0 | 0 |

#### 3. M.S.P. of Rahu

| | M | D | H |
|---|---|---|---|
| Rahu | 2 | 21 | 0 |
| Jupiter | 2 | 12 | 0 |
| Saturn | 2 | 25 | 12 |
| Mercury | 2 | 16 | 12 |
| Ketu | 1 | 1 | 12 |
| Venus | 3 | 0 | 12 |
| Sun | 0 | 27 | 0 |
| Moon | 1 | 15 | 0 |
| Mars | 1 | 1 | 0 |
| Total | 18 | 0 | 0 |

## 4. M.S.P. of Jupiter

|  | M | D | H |
|---|---|---|---|
| Jupiter | 2 | 4 | 0 |
| Saturn | 2 | 16 | 0 |
| Mercury | 2 | 8 | 0 |
| Ketu | 0 | 28 | 0 |
| Venus | 2 | 20 | 0 |
| Sun | 0 | 24 | 0 |
| Moon | 1 | 10 | 0 |
| Mars | 0 | 28 | 0 |
| Rahu | 2 | 12 | 0 |
| **Total** | **16** | **0** | **0** |

## 5. M.S.P. of Saturn

|  | M | D | H |
|---|---|---|---|
| Saturn | 3 | 0 | 6 |
| Mercury | 2 | 20 | 18 |
| Ketu | 1 | 3 | 6 |
| Venus | 3 | 5 | 0 |
| Sun | 0 | 28 | 12 |
| Moon | 1 | 17 | 12 |
| Mars | 1 | 3 | 6 |
| Rahu | 2 | 25 | 12 |
| Jupiter | 2 | 16 | 0 |
| **Total** | **19** | **0** | **0** |

## 6. M.S.P. of Mercury

|  | M | D | H |
|---|---|---|---|
| Mercury | 2 | 12 | 6 |
| Ketu | 0 | 29 | 18 |
| Venus | 2 | 25 | 0 |
| Sun | 0 | 25 | 12 |
| Moon | 1 | 12 | 12 |
| Mars | 0 | 29 | 18 |
| Rahu | 2 | 16 | 12 |
| Jupiter | 2 | 8 | 0 |
| Saturn | 2 | 20 | 18 |
| **Total** | **17** | **0** | **0** |

## 7. M.S.P. of Ketu

|  | M | D | H |
|---|---|---|---|
| Ketu | 0 | 12 | 6 |
| Venus | 1 | 5 | 0 |
| Sun | 0 | 10 | 12 |
| Moon | 0 | 17 | 12 |
| Mars | 0 | 12 | 6 |
| Rahu | 1 | 1 | 12 |
| Jupiter | 0 | 28 | 0 |
| Saturn | 1 | 3 | 6 |
| Mercury | 0 | 29 | 18 |
| **Total** | **7** | **0** | **0** |

## 8. M.S.P. of Venus

|  | M | D | H |
|---|---|---|---|
| Venus | 3 | 10 | 0 |
| Sun | 1 | 0 | 0 |
| Moon | 1 | 20 | 0 |
| Mars | 1 | 5 | 0 |
| Rahu | 3 | 0 | 0 |
| Jupiter | 2 | 20 | 0 |
| Saturn | 3 | 5 | 0 |
| Mercury | 2 | 25 | 0 |
| Ketu | 1 | 5 | 0 |
| **Total** | **20** | **0** | **0** |

## 9. M.S.P. of Sun

|  | M | D | H |
|---|---|---|---|
| Sun | 0 | 9 | 0 |
| Moon | 0 | 15 | 0 |
| Mars | 0 | 10 | 12 |
| Rahu | 0 | 27 | 0 |
| Jupiter | 0 | 24 | 0 |
| Saturn | 0 | 28 | 12 |
| Mercury | 0 | 25 | 12 |
| Ketu | 0 | 10 | 12 |
| Venus | 1 | 0 | 0 |
| **Total** | **6** | **0** | **0** |

# MAR'S PERIODS

## Sub-Periods

| | Mars | Juptier | Saturn | Mercury | Ketu | Venus | Sun | Moon | Total |
|---|---|---|---|---|---|---|---|---|---|
| Years | 0 | 0 | 1 | 0 | 0 | 1 | 0 | 0 | 7 |
| Months | 4 | 11 | 1 | 11 | 4 | 2 | 4 | 7 | 0 |
| Days | 27 | 6 | 9 | 27 | 27 | 0 | 6 | 0 | 0 |

## Minor Sub-periods

### 1. M.S.P. of Mars

| | M | D | H |
|---|---|---|---|
| Mars | 0 | 8 | 13.8 |
| Rahu | 0 | 22 | 1.2 |
| Jupiter | 0 | 19 | 14.4 |
| Saturn | 0 | 23 | 6.6 |
| Mercury | 0 | 20 | 19.8 |
| Ketu | 0 | 8 | 13.8 |
| Venus | 0 | 24 | 12.0 |
| Sun | 0 | 7 | 8.4 |
| Moon | 0 | 12 | 6.0 |
| **Total** | **4** | **27** | **0.0** |

### 2. M.S.P. of Rahu

| | M | D | H |
|---|---|---|---|
| Rahu | 1 | 26 | 13.8 |
| Jupiter | 1 | 20 | 9.6 |
| Saturn | 1 | 29 | 20.4 |
| Mercury | 1 | 23 | 13.2 |
| Ketu | 0 | 22 | 1.2 |
| Venus | 2 | 3 | 0.0 |
| Sun | 0 | 18 | 21.6 |
| Moon | 1 | 1 | 12.0 |
| Mars | 0 | 22 | 1.2 |
| **Total** | **12** | **18** | **0.0** |

### 3. M.S.P. of Jupiter

| | M | D | H |
|---|---|---|---|
| Jupiter | 1 | 14 | 19.2 |
| Saturn | 1 | 23 | 4.8 |
| Mercury | 1 | 17 | 14.4 |
| Ketu | 0 | 19 | 14.4 |
| Venus | 1 | 26 | 0.0 |
| Sun | 0 | 16 | 19.2 |
| Moon | 0 | 28 | 0.0 |
| Mars | 0 | 19 | 14.4 |
| Rahu | 1 | 20 | 9.6 |
| **Total** | **11** | **6** | **0.0** |

## 4. M.S.P. of Saturn

| | M | D | H |
|---|---|---|---|
| Saturn | 2 | 3 | 4.2 |
| Mercury | 1 | 26 | 12.6 |
| Ketu | 0 | 23 | 6.6 |
| Venus | 2 | 6 | 12.0 |
| Sun | 0 | 19 | 22.8 |
| Moon | 1 | 3 | 6.0 |
| Mars | 0 | 23 | 6.6 |
| Rahu | 1 | 29 | 20.4 |
| Jupiter | 1 | 23 | 4.8 |
| **Total** | **13** | **9** | **0.0** |

## 5. M.S.P. of Mercury

| | M | D | H |
|---|---|---|---|
| Mercury | 1 | 20 | 18.8 |
| Ketu | 0 | 20 | 19.8 |
| Venus | 1 | 29 | 12.0 |
| Sun | 0 | 17 | 20.4 |
| Moon | 0 | 29 | 18.0 |
| Mars | 0 | 20 | 19.8 |
| Rahu | 1 | 23 | 13.2 |
| Jupiter | 1 | 17 | 14.4 |
| Saturn | 1 | 26 | 12.6 |
| **Total** | **11** | **27** | **0.0** |

## 6. M.S.P. of Ketu

| | M | D | H |
|---|---|---|---|
| Ketu | 0 | 8 | 13.8 |
| Venus | 0 | 24 | 12.0 |
| Sun | 0 | 7 | 8.4 |
| Moon | 0 | 12 | 6.0 |
| Mars | 0 | 8 | 13.8 |
| Rahu | 1 | 22 | 1.2 |
| Jupiter | 0 | 19 | 14.4 |
| Saturn | 0 | 23 | 6.6 |
| Mercury | 0 | 20 | 19.8 |
| **Total** | **4** | **27** | **0.0** |

## 7. M.S.P. of Venus

| | M | D | H |
|---|---|---|---|
| Venus | 2 | 10 | 0 |
| Sun | 0 | 21 | 0 |
| Moon | 1 | 5 | 0 |
| Mars | 0 | 24 | 12 |
| Rahu | 2 | 3 | 0 |
| Jupiter | 1 | 26 | 0 |
| Saturn | 2 | 6 | 12 |
| Mercury | 1 | 29 | 12 |
| Ketu | 0 | 24 | 12 |
| **Total** | **14** | **0** | **0** |

## 8. M.S.P. of Sun

| | M | D | H |
|---|---|---|---|
| Sun | 0 | 6 | 7.2 |
| Moon | 0 | 10 | 12.0 |
| Mars | 0 | 7 | 8.4 |
| Rahu | 0 | 18 | 21.6 |
| Jupiter | 0 | 16 | 19.2 |
| Saturn | 0 | 19 | 22.8 |
| Mercury | 0 | 17 | 20.4 |
| Ketu | 0 | 7 | 8.4 |
| Venus | 0 | 21 | 0.0 |
| **Total** | **4** | **6** | **0.0** |

## 9. M.S.P. of Moon

| | M | D | H |
|---|---|---|---|
| Moon | 0 | 17 | 12 |
| Mars | 0 | 12 | 6 |
| Rahu | 1 | 1 | 12 |
| Jupiter | 0 | 28 | 0 |
| Saturn | 1 | 3 | 6 |
| Mercury | 0 | 29 | 18 |
| Ketu | 0 | 12 | 6 |
| Venus | 1 | 5 | 0 |
| Sun | 0 | 10 | 12 |
| **Total** | **7** | **0** | **0** |

# RAHU'S PERIODS

## Sub-Periods

| | Rahu | Juptier | Saturn | Mercury | Ketu | Venus | Sun | Moon | Mars | Total |
|---|---|---|---|---|---|---|---|---|---|---|
| Years | 2 | 2 | 2 | 2 | 1 | 3 | 0 | 1 | 1 | 18 |
| Months | 8 | 4 | 10 | 6 | 0 | 0 | 10 | 6 | 0 | 0 |
| Days | 12 | 24 | 6 | 18 | 18 | 0 | 24 | 0 | 18 | 0 |

## Minor Sub-periods

### 1. M.S.P. of Rahu

| | M | D | H |
|---|---|---|---|
| Rahu | 4 | 25 | 19.2 |
| Jupiter | 4 | 19 | 14.4 |
| Saturn | 5 | 3 | 21.6 |
| Mercury | 4 | 17 | 16.8 |
| Ketu | 1 | 26 | 16.8 |
| Venus | 5 | 12 | 0.0 |
| Sun | 1 | 18 | 14.4 |
| Moon | 2 | 21 | -0.0 |
| Mars | 1 | 26 | 16.8 |
| Total | 32 | 12 | 0.0 |

### 2. M.S.P. of Jupiter

| | M | D | H |
|---|---|---|---|
| Jupiter | 3 | 25 | 4.8 |
| Saturn | 4 | 16 | 19.2 |
| Mercury | 4 | 2 | 9.6 |
| Ketu | 1 | 20 | 9.6 |
| Venus | 6 | 24 | 0.0 |
| Sun | 1 | 13 | 4.8 |
| Moon | 2 | 12 | 0.0 |
| Mars | 1 | 20 | 9.6 |
| Rahu | 4 | 19 | 14.4 |
| Total | 28 | 24 | 0.0 |

### 3. M.S.P. of Saturn

| | M | D | H |
|---|---|---|---|
| Saturn | 5 | 12 | 10.8 |
| Mercury | 4 | 25 | 8.4 |
| Ketu | 1 | 29 | 20.4 |
| Venus | 5 | 21 | 0.0 |
| Sun | 1 | 21 | 7.2 |
| Moon | 2 | 25 | 12.0 |
| Mars | 1 | 29 | 20.4 |
| Rahu | 5 | 3 | 21.6 |
| Jupiter | 4 | 16 | 19.2 |
| Total | 34 | 6 | 0.0 |

| 4. M.S.P. of Mercury | M | D | H |
|---|---|---|---|
| Mercury | 4 | 10 | 1.2 |
| Ketu | 1 | 23 | 13.2 |
| Venus | 5 | 3 | 0.0 |
| Sun | 1 | 15 | 21.6 |
| Moon | 2 | 16 | 12.0 |
| Mars | 1 | 23 | 13.2 |
| Rahu | 4 | 17 | 16.8 |
| Jupiter | 4 | 2 | 9.6 |
| Saturn | 4 | 25 | 8.4 |
| **Total** | **30** | **18** | **0.0** |

| 7. M.S.P. of Sun | M | D | H |
|---|---|---|---|
| Sun | 0 | 16 | 4.8 |
| Moon | 0 | 27 | 0.0 |
| Mars | 0 | 18 | 21.6 |
| Rahu | 1 | 18 | 14.4 |
| Jupiter | 1 | 13 | 4.8 |
| Saturn | 1 | 21 | 7.2 |
| Mercury | 1 | 15 | 21.6 |
| Ketu | 0 | 18 | 21.6 |
| Venus | 1 | 24 | 0.0 |
| **Total** | **10** | **24** | **0.0** |

| 5. M.S.P. of Ketu | M | D | H |
|---|---|---|---|
| Ketu | 0 | 22 | 1.2 |
| Venus | 2 | 3 | 0.0 |
| Sun | 0 | 18 | 21.6 |
| Moon | 1 | 1 | 12.0 |
| Mars | 0 | 22 | 1.2 |
| Rahu | 1 | 26 | 16.8 |
| Jupiter | 1 | 20 | 9.6 |
| Saturn | 1 | 29 | 20.4 |
| Mercury | 1 | 23 | 13.2 |
| **Total** | **12** | **18** | **0.0** |

| 8. M.S.P. of Moon | M | D | H |
|---|---|---|---|
| Moon | 1 | 15 | 0 |
| Mars | 1 | 1 | 12 |
| Rahu | 2 | 21 | 0 |
| Jupiter | 2 | 12 | 0 |
| Saturn | 2 | 25 | 12 |
| Mercury | 2 | 16 | 12 |
| Ketu | 1 | 1 | 12 |
| Venus | 3 | 0 | 0 |
| Sun | 0 | 27 | 0 |
| **Total** | **18** | **0** | **0** |

| 6. M.S.P. of Venus | M | D | H |
|---|---|---|---|
| Venus | 6 | 0 | 0 |
| Sun | 1 | 24 | 0 |
| Moon | 3 | 0 | 0 |
| Mars | 2 | 3 | 0 |
| Rahu | 5 | 12 | 0 |
| Jupiter | 4 | 24 | 0 |
| Saturn | 5 | 21 | 0 |
| Mercury | 5 | 3 | 0 |
| Ketu | 2 | 3 | 0 |
| **Total** | **36** | **0** | **0** |

| 9. M.S.P. of Mars | M | D | H |
|---|---|---|---|
| Mars | 0 | 22 | 1.2 |
| Rahu | 1 | 26 | 16.8 |
| Jupiter | 1 | 20 | 9.6 |
| Saturn | 1 | 29 | 20.4 |
| Mercury | 1 | 23 | 13.2 |
| Ketu | 0 | 22 | 1.2 |
| Venus | 2 | 3 | 0.0 |
| Sun | 0 | 18 | 21.6 |
| Moon | 1 | 1 | 12.0 |
| **Total** | **12** | **18** | **00.0** |

# JUPITER'S PERIODS

## Sub-Periods

|  | Jupiter | Saturn | Mercury | Ketu | Venus | Sun | Moon | Mars | Rahu | Total |
|---|---|---|---|---|---|---|---|---|---|---|
| Years | 2 | 2 | 2 | 0 | 2 | 0 | 1 | 0 | 2 | 16 |
| Months | 1 | 6 | 3 | 11 | 8 | 9 | 4 | 11 | 4 | 0 |
| Days | 18 | 12 | 6 | 6 | 0 | 18 | 0 | 6 | 24 | 0 |

## Minor Sub-periods

### 1. M.S.P. of Jupiter

|  | M | D | H |
|---|---|---|---|
| Jupiter | 3 | 12 | 9.6 |
| Saturn | 4 | 1 | 14.4 |
| Mercury | 3 | 18 | 19.2 |
| Ketu | 1 | 14 | 19.2 |
| Venus | 4 | 8 | 0.0 |
| Sun | 1 | 8 | 9.6 |
| Moon | 2 | 4 | 0.0 |
| Mars | 1 | 14 | 19.2 |
| Rahu | 3 | 25 | 4.8 |
| Total | 25 | 18 | 0.0 |

### 2. M.S.P. of Saturn

|  | M | D | H |
|---|---|---|---|
| Saturn | 4 | 24 | 9.6 |
| Mercury | 4 | 9 | 4.8 |
| Ketu | 1 | 23 | 4.8 |
| Venus | 5 | 2 | 0.0 |
| Sun | 1 | 15 | 14.4 |
| Moon | 2 | 16 | 0.0 |
| Mars | 1 | 23 | 4.8 |
| Rahu | 4 | 16 | 19.2 |
| Jupiter | 4 | 1 | 14.4 |
| Total | 30 | 12 | 0.0 |

### 3. M.S.P. of Mercury

|  | M | D | H |
|---|---|---|---|
| Mercury | 3 | 25 | 14.4 |
| Ketu | 1 | 17 | 14.4 |
| Venus | 4 | 16 | 0.0 |
| Sun | 1 | 10 | 19.2 |
| Moon | 2 | 8 | 0.0 |
| Mars | 1 | 17 | 14.4 |
| Rahu | 4 | 2 | 9.6 |
| Jupiter | 3 | 18 | 19.2 |
| Saturn | 4 | 9 | 4.8 |
| Total | 27 | 6 | 0.0 |

## 4. M.S.P. of Ketu

| | M | D | H |
|---|---|---|---|
| Ketu | 0 | 19 | 14.4 |
| Venus | 1 | 26 | 0.0 |
| Sun | 0 | 16 | 19.2 |
| Moon | 0 | 28 | 0.0 |
| Mars | 0 | 19 | 14.4 |
| Rahu | 1 | 20 | 9.6 |
| Jupiter | 1 | 14 | 19.2 |
| Saturn | 1 | 23 | 4.8 |
| Mercury | 1 | 17 | 14.4 |
| **Total** | **11** | **6** | **0.0** |

## 5. M.S.P. of Venus

| | M | D | H |
|---|---|---|---|
| Venus | 5 | 10 | 0.0 |
| Sun | 1 | 18 | 0.0 |
| Moon | 2 | 20 | 0.0 |
| Mars | 1 | 26 | 0.0 |
| Rahu | 4 | 24 | 0.0 |
| Jupiter | 4 | 8 | 0.0 |
| Saturn | 5 | 2 | 0.0 |
| Mercury | 4 | 6 | 0.0 |
| Ketu | 1 | 26 | 0.0 |
| **Total** | **32** | **0** | **0.0** |

## 6. M.S.P. of Sun

| | M | D | H |
|---|---|---|---|
| Sun | 0 | 14 | 9.6 |
| Moon | 0 | 24 | 0.0 |
| Mars | 0 | 16 | 19.2 |
| Rahu | 1 | 13 | 4.8 |
| Jupiter | 1 | 8 | 9.6 |
| Saturn | 1 | 15 | 14.4 |
| Mercury | 1 | 10 | 19.2 |
| Ketu | 0 | 16 | 19.2 |
| Venus | 1 | 18 | 0.0 |
| **Total** | **9** | **8** | **0.0** |

## 7. M.S.P. of Moon

| | M | D | H |
|---|---|---|---|
| Moon | 1 | 10 | 0.0 |
| Mars | 0 | 28 | 0.0 |
| Rahu | 2 | 12 | 0.0 |
| Jupiter | 2 | 4 | 0.0 |
| Saturn | 2 | 16 | 0.0 |
| Mercury | 2 | 8 | 0.0 |
| Ketu | 0 | 28 | 0.0 |
| Venus | 2 | 20 | 0.0 |
| Sun | 0 | 24 | 0.0 |
| **Total** | **16** | **0** | **0.0** |

## 8. M.S.P. of Mars

| | M | D | H |
|---|---|---|---|
| Mars | 0 | 19 | 14.4 |
| Rahu | 1 | 20 | 14.4 |
| Jupiter | 1 | 14 | 19.2 |
| Saturn | 1 | 23 | 4.8 |
| Mercury | 1 | 17 | 14.4 |
| Ketu | 1 | 19 | 14.4 |
| Venus | 1 | 26 | 0.0 |
| Sun | 0 | 16 | 19.2 |
| Moon | 0 | 28 | 0.0 |
| **Total** | **11** | **6** | **0.0** |

## 9. M.S.P. of Rahu

| | M | D | H |
|---|---|---|---|
| Rahu | 4 | 19 | 14.4 |
| Jupiter | 3 | 25 | 4.8 |
| Saturn | 4 | 16 | 19.2 |
| Mercury | 4 | 2 | 9.6 |
| Ketu | 1 | 20 | 9.6 |
| Venus | 4 | 24 | 0.0 |
| Sun | 1 | 13 | 4.8 |
| Moon | 2 | 12 | 0.0 |
| Mars | 1 | 20 | 9.6 |
| **Total** | **28** | **24** | **0.0** |

## SATURN'S PERIODS

### Sub-Periods

| | Saturn | Mercury | Ketu | Venus | Sun | Moon | Mars | Rahu | Juptier | Total |
|---|---|---|---|---|---|---|---|---|---|---|
| Years | 3 | 2 | 1 | 3 | 0 | 1 | 1 | 2 | 2 | 19 |
| Months | 0 | 8 | 1 | 2 | 11 | 7 | 1 | 10 | 6 | 0 |
| Days | 3 | 9 | 9 | 0 | 12 | 0 | 9 | 6 | 12 | 0 |

### Minor Sub-periods

#### 1. M.S.P. of Saturn

| | M | D | H |
|---|---|---|---|
| Saturn | 5 | 21 | 11.4 |
| Mercury | 5 | 3 | 10.2 |
| Ketu | 2 | 3 | 4.2 |
| Venus | 6 | 0 | 12.0 |
| Sun | 1 | 24 | 3.6 |
| Moon | 3 | 0 | 6.0 |
| Mars | 2 | 3 | 4.2 |
| Rahu | 5 | 12 | 10.8 |
| Jupiter | 4 | 24 | 9.6 |
| **Total** | **36** | **3** | **0.0** |

#### 2. M.S.P. of Mercury

| | M | D | H |
|---|---|---|---|
| Mercury | 4 | 17 | 6.6 |
| Ketu | 1 | 26 | 12.6 |
| Venus | 5 | 11 | 12.0 |
| Sun | 1 | 18 | 10.8 |
| Moon | 2 | 20 | 18.0 |
| Mars | 1 | 26 | 12.6 |
| Rahu | 4 | 25 | 8.4 |
| Jupiter | 4 | 9 | 4.8 |
| Saturn | 4 | 3 | 10.2 |
| **Total** | **32** | **9** | **0.0** |

#### 3. M.S.P. of Ketu

| | M | D | H |
|---|---|---|---|
| Ketu | 0 | 23 | 6.6 |
| Venus | 2 | 6 | 12.0 |
| Sun | 0 | 19 | 22.8 |
| Moon | 1 | 3 | 6.0 |
| Mars | 0 | 23 | 6.6 |
| Rahu | 1 | 29 | 20.4 |
| Jupiter | 1 | 23 | 4.8 |
| Saturn | 2 | 3 | 4.2 |
| Mercury | 1 | 26 | 12.6 |
| **Total** | **13** | **9** | **0.0** |

**4. M.S.P. of Venus**

| | M | D | H |
|---|---|---|---|
| Venus | 6 | 10 | 0.0 |
| Sun | 1 | 27 | 0.0 |
| Moon | 3 | 5 | 0.0 |
| Mars | 2 | 6 | 12.0 |
| Rahu | 5 | 21 | 0.0 |
| Jupiter | 5 | 2 | 0.0 |
| Saturn | 6 | 0 | 12.0 |
| Mercury | 5 | 11 | 12.0 |
| Ketu | 2 | 6 | 12.0 |
| **Total** | **38** | **0** | **0.0** |

**5. M.S.P. of Sun**

| | M | D | H |
|---|---|---|---|
| Sun | 0 | 17 | 2.4 |
| Moon | 0 | 28 | 12.0 |
| Mars | 0 | 19 | 22.8 |
| Rahu | 1 | 21 | 1.2 |
| Jupiter | 1 | 15 | 14.4 |
| Saturn | 1 | 24 | 3.6 |
| Mercury | 1 | 18 | 10.8 |
| Ketu | 0 | 19 | 22.8 |
| Venus | 1 | 27 | 0.0 |
| **Total** | **11** | **12** | **0.0** |

**6. M.S.P. of Moon**

| | M | D | H |
|---|---|---|---|
| Moon | 1 | 17 | 12.0 |
| Mars | 1 | 3 | 6.0 |
| Rahu | 2 | 25 | 12.0 |
| Jupiter | 2 | 16 | 0.0 |
| Saturn | 3 | 0 | 6.0 |
| Mercury | 2 | 20 | 18.0 |
| Ketu | 1 | 3 | 6.0 |
| Venus | 3 | 5 | 0.0 |
| Sun | 0 | 28 | 12.0 |
| **Total** | **19** | **0** | **0.0** |

**7. M.S.P. of Mars**

| | M | D | H |
|---|---|---|---|
| Mars | 0 | 23 | 6.6 |
| Rahu | 1 | 29 | 20.4 |
| Jupiter | 1 | 23 | 4.8 |
| Saturn | 2 | 3 | 4.2 |
| Mercury | 1 | 26 | 12.6 |
| Ketu | 0 | 23 | 6.6 |
| Venus | 2 | 6 | 12.0 |
| Sun | 0 | 19 | 22.8 |
| Moon | 1 | 3 | 6.0 |
| **Total** | **13** | **9** | **0.0** |

**8. M.S.P. of Rahu**

| | M | D | H |
|---|---|---|---|
| Rahu | 5 |  | 21.6 |
| Jupiter | 4 | 16 | 19.2 |
| Saturn | 5 | 12 | 10.8 |
| Mercury | 4 | 25 | 8.4 |
| Ketu | 1 | 29 | 20.4 |
| Venus | 5 | 21 | 0.0 |
| Sun | 1 | 21 | 7.2 |
| Moon | 2 | 25 | 12.0 |
| Mars | 1 | 29 | 20.4 |
| **Total** | **34** | **6** | **0.0** |

**9. M.S.P. of Jupiter**

| | M | D | H |
|---|---|---|---|
| Jupiter | 4 | 1 | 14.4 |
| Saturn | 4 | 24 | 9.6 |
| Mercury | 4 | 9 | 4.8 |
| Ketu | 1 | 23 | 4.8 |
| Venus | 5 | 2 | 0.0 |
| Sun | 1 | 15 | 14.4 |
| Moon | 2 | 16 | 0.0 |
| Mars | 1 | 23 | 4.8 |
| Rahu | 4 | 16 | 19.2 |
| **Total** | **30** | **12** | **0.0** |

# MERCURY'S PERIODS

## Sub-Periods

|  | Mercury | Ketu | Venus | Sun | Moon | Mars | Rahu | Jupiter | Saturn | Total |
|---|---|---|---|---|---|---|---|---|---|---|
| Years | 2 | 0 | 2 | 0 | 1 | 0 | 2 | 2 | 2 | 17 |
| Months | 4 | 11 | 10 | 10 | 5 | 11 | 6 | 3 | 8 | 0 |
| Days | 27 | 27 | 0 | 6 | 0 | 27 | 18 | 6 | 9 | 0 |

## Minor Sub-periods

### 1. M.S.P. of Mercury

|  | M | D | H |
|---|---|---|---|
| Mercury | 4 | 2 | 19.8 |
| Ketu | 1 | 20 | 13.8 |
| Venus | 4 | 24 | 12.0 |
| Sun | 1 | 13 | 3.4 |
| Moon | 2 | 12 | 6.0 |
| Mars | 1 | 20 | 13.8 |
| Rahu | 4 | 10 | 1.2 |
| Jupiter | 3 | 25 | 14.4 |
| Saturn | 4 | 17 | 6.6 |
| Total | 28 | 27 | 0.0 |

### 2. M.S.P. of Ketu

|  | M | D | H |
|---|---|---|---|
| Ketu | 0 | 20 | 19.8 |
| Venus | 1 | 29 | 12.0 |
| Sun | 0 | 17 | 20.4 |
| Moon | 0 | 29 | 18.0 |
| Mars | 0 | 20 | 19.8 |
| Rahu | 1 | 23 | 13.2 |
| Jupiter | 1 | 17 | 14.4 |
| Saturn | 1 | 26 | 12.6 |
| Mercury | 1 | 20 | 13.8 |
| Total | 11 | 27 | 0.0 |

### 3. M.S.P. of Venus

|  | M | D | H |
|---|---|---|---|
| Venus | 5 | 20 | 0.0 |
| Sun | 1 | 21 | 0.0 |
| Moon | 2 | 25 | 0.0 |
| Mars | 1 | 29 | 12.0 |
| Rahu | 5 | 3 | 0.0 |
| Jupiter | 4 | 16 | 0.0 |
| Saturn | 5 | 11 | 12.0 |
| Mercury | 4 | 24 | 12.0 |
| Ketu | 1 | 20 | 12.0 |
| Total | 34 | 0 | 0.0 |

## 4. M.S.P. of Sun

|         | M  | D  | H    |
|---------|----|----|------|
| Sun     | 0  | 15 | 7.2  |
| Moon    | 0  | 25 | 12.0 |
| Mars    | 0  | 17 | 20.4 |
| Rahu    | 1  | 15 | 21.6 |
| Jupiter | 1  | 10 | 19.2 |
| Saturn  | 1  | 18 | 10.8 |
| Mercury | 1  | 13 | 8.4  |
| Ketu    | 0  | 17 | 20.4 |
| Venus   | 1  | 21 | 0.0  |
| Total   | 10 | 6  | 0.0  |

## 5. M.S.P. of Moon

|         | M  | D  | H  |
|---------|----|----|----|
| Moon    | 1  | 12 | 12 |
| Mars    | 0  | 29 | 18 |
| Rahu    | 2  | 16 | 12 |
| Jupiter | 2  | 8  | 0  |
| Saturn  | 2  | 20 | 18 |
| Mercury | 2  | 12 | 6  |
| Ketu    | 0  | 29 | 18 |
| Venus   | 2  | 25 | 0  |
| Sun     | 0  | 25 | 12 |
| Total   | 17 | 0  | 0  |

## 6. M.S.P. of Mars

|         | M  | D  | H    |
|---------|----|----|------|
| Mars    | 0  | 20 | 19.8 |
| Rahu    | 1  | 23 | 13.2 |
| Jupiter | 1  | 17 | 14.4 |
| Saturn  | 1  | 26 | 12.6 |
| Mercury | 1  | 20 | 13.8 |
| Ketu    | 0  | 20 | 19.8 |
| Venus   | 1  | 29 | 12.0 |
| Sun     | 0  | 17 | 20.4 |
| Moon    | 0  | 29 | 18.0 |
| Total   | 11 | 27 | 0.0  |

## 7. M.S.P. of Rahu

|         | M  | D  | H    |
|---------|----|----|------|
| Rahu    | 4  | 17 | 16.8 |
| Jupiter | 4  | 2  | 9.6  |
| Saturn  | 4  | 25 | 8.4  |
| Mercury | 4  | 10 | 1.2  |
| Ketu    | 1  | 23 | 13.2 |
| Venus   | 5  | 3  | 0.0  |
| Sun     | 1  | 15 | 21.6 |
| Moon    | 2  | 16 | 12.0 |
| Mars    | 1  | 23 | 13.2 |
| Total   | 30 | 18 | 0.0  |

## 8. M.S.P. of Jupiter

|         | M  | D  | H    |
|---------|----|----|------|
| Jupiter | 3  | 18 | 19.2 |
| Saturn  | 4  | 9  | 4.8  |
| Mercury | 3  | 25 | 14.4 |
| Ketu    | 1  | 17 | 14.4 |
| Venus   | 4  | 16 | 0.0  |
| Sun     | 1  | 10 | 19.2 |
| Moon    | 2  | 8  | 0.0  |
| Mars    | 1  | 17 | 14.4 |
| Rahu    | 4  | 2  | 9.6  |
| Total   | 27 | 6  | 0.0  |

## 9. M.S.P. of Saturn

|         | M  | D  | H    |
|---------|----|----|------|
| Saturn  | 5  | 3  | 10.2 |
| Mercury | 4  | 17 | 6.6  |
| Ketu    | 1  | 26 | 12.6 |
| Venus   | 5  | 11 | 12.0 |
| Sun     | 1  | 18 | 10.8 |
| Moon    | 2  | 20 | 18.0 |
| Mars    | 1  | 26 | 12.6 |
| Rahu    | 4  | 25 | 8.4  |
| Jupiter | 4  | 9  | 4.8  |
| Total   | 32 | 9  | 0.0  |

## KETU'S PERIODS

### Sub-Periods

| | Ketu | Venus | Sun | Moon | Mars | Rahu | Juptier | Saturn | Mercury | Total |
|---|---|---|---|---|---|---|---|---|---|---|
| Years | 0 | 1 | 0 | 0 | 0 | 1 | 0 | 1 | 0 | 7 |
| Months | 4 | 2 | 4 | 7 | 4 | 0 | 11 | 1 | 11 | 0 |
| Days | 27 | 0 | 6 | 0 | 27 | 18 | 6 | 9 | 27 | 0 |

### Minor Sub-periods

#### 1. M.S.P. of Ketu

| | M | D | H |
|---|---|---|---|
| Ketu | 0 | 8 | 13.8 |
| Venus | 0 | 24 | 12.0 |
| Sun | 0 | 7 | 8.4 |
| Moon | 0 | 12 | 6.0 |
| Mars | 0 | 8 | 13.8 |
| Rahu | 0 | 22 | 1.2 |
| Jupiter | 0 | 19 | 14.4 |
| Saturn | 0 | 23 | 6.6 |
| Mercury | 0 | 20 | 19.8 |
| Total | 4 | 27 | 0.0 |

#### 2. M.S.P. of Venus

| | M | D | H |
|---|---|---|---|
| Venus | 2 | 10 | 0 |
| Sun | 0 | 21 | 0 |
| Moon | 1 | 5 | 0 |
| Mars | 0 | 24 | 12 |
| Rahu | 2 | 3 | 0 |
| Jupiter | 1 | 26 | 0 |
| Saturn | 2 | 6 | 12 |
| Mercury | 1 | 29 | 12 |
| Ketu | 0 | 24 | 12 |
| Total | 14 | 0 | 0 |

#### 3. M.S.P. of Sun

| | M | D | H |
|---|---|---|---|
| Sun | 0 | 6 | 7.2 |
| Moon | 0 | 10 | 12.0 |
| Mars | 0 | 7 | 8.4 |
| Rahu | 0 | 18 | 21.6 |
| Jupiter | 0 | 16 | 19.2 |
| Saturn | 0 | 19 | 22.8 |
| Mercury | 0 | 17 | 20.4 |
| Ketu | 0 | 7 | 8.4 |
| Venus | 0 | 21 | 0.0 |
| Total | 4 | 6 | 0.0 |

## 4. M.S.P. of Moon

| | M | D | H |
|---|---|---|---|
| Moon | 0 | 17 | 12.0 |
| Mars | 0 | 12 | 6.0 |
| Rahu | 1 | 1 | 12.0 |
| Jupiter | 0 | 28 | 0.0 |
| Saturn | 1 | 3 | 6.0 |
| Mercury | 0 | 29 | 18.0 |
| Ketu | 0 | 12 | 6.0 |
| Venus | 1 | 5 | 0.0 |
| Sun | 0 | 10 | 12.0 |
| Total | 7 | 0 | 0.0 |

## 5. M.S.P. of Mars

| | M | D | H |
|---|---|---|---|
| Mars | 0 | 8 | 13.8 |
| Rahu | 0 | 22 | 1.2 |
| Jupiter | 0 | 19 | 14.4 |
| Saturn | 0 | 23 | 6.6 |
| Mercury | 0 | 20 | 19.8 |
| Ketu | 0 | 8 | 13.8 |
| Venus | 0 | 24 | 12.0 |
| Sun | 0 | 7 | 8.4 |
| Moon | 0 | 12 | 6.0 |
| Total | 4 | 27 | 0.0 |

## 6. M.S.P. of Rahu

| | M | D | H |
|---|---|---|---|
| Rahu | 1 | 26 | 16.8 |
| Jupiter | 1 | 20 | 9.6 |
| Saturn | 1 | 29 | 20.4 |
| Mercury | 1 | 23 | 13.2 |
| Ketu | 0 | 22 | 1.2 |
| Venus | 2 | 3 | 0.0 |
| Sun | 0 | 18 | 21.6 |
| Moon | 1 | 1 | 12.0 |
| Mars | 0 | 22 | 1.2 |
| Total | 12 | 18 | 0.0 |

## 7. M.S.P. of Jupiter

| | M | D | H |
|---|---|---|---|
| Jupiter | 1 | 14 | 19.2 |
| Saturn | 1 | 23 | 4.8 |
| Mercury | 1 | 17 | 14.4 |
| Ketu | 0 | 19 | 14.4 |
| Venus | 1 | 26 | 0.0 |
| Sun | 0 | 16 | 19.2 |
| Moon | 0 | 28 | 0.0 |
| Mars | 0 | 19 | 14.4 |
| Rahu | 1 | 20 | 9.6 |
| Total | 11 | 6 | 0.0 |

## 8. M.S.P. of Saturn

| | M | D | H |
|---|---|---|---|
| Saturn | 2 | 3 | 4.2 |
| Mercury | 1 | 26 | 12.6 |
| Ketu | 0 | 23 | 6.6 |
| Venus | 2 | 6 | 12.0 |
| Sun | 0 | 19 | 22.8 |
| Moon | 1 | 3 | 6.0 |
| Mars | 0 | 23 | 6.5 |
| Rahu | 1 | 19 | 20.4 |
| Jupiter | 1 | 23 | 4.8 |
| Total | 13 | 9 | 0.0 |

## 9. M.S.P. of Mercury

| | M | D | H |
|---|---|---|---|
| Mercury | 1 | 20 | 13.8 |
| Ketu | 0 | 20 | 19.8 |
| Venus | 1 | 29 | 12.0 |
| Sun | 0 | 17 | 20.4 |
| Moon | 0 | 29 | 18.0 |
| Mars | 0 | 20 | 19.8 |
| Rahu | 1 | 23 | 13.2 |
| Jupiter | 1 | 17 | 14.4 |
| Saturn | 1 | 26 | 12.6 |
| Total | 11 | 27 | 0.0 |

# VENUS'S PERIODS

## Sub-Periods

| | Venus | Sun | Moon | Mars | Rahu | Juptier | Saturn | Mercury | Ketu | Total |
|---|---|---|---|---|---|---|---|---|---|---|
| Years | 3 | 1 | 1 | 1 | 3 | 2 | 3 | 2 | 1 | 20 |
| Months | 4 | 0 | 8 | 2 | 0 | 8 | 2 | 10 | 2 | 0 |
| Days | 0 | 0 | 0 | 0 | 0 | 0 | 0 | 0 | 0 | 0 |

## Minor Sub-periods

### 1. M.S.P. of Venus

| | M | D | H |
|---|---|---|---|
| Venus | 6 | 20 | 0 |
| Sun | 2 | 0 | 0 |
| Moon | 3 | 10 | 0 |
| Mars | 2 | 10 | 0 |
| Rahu | 6 | 0 | 0 |
| Jupiter | 5 | 10 | 0 |
| Saturn | 6 | 10 | 0 |
| Mercury | 5 | 20 | 0 |
| Ketu | 2 | 10 | 0 |
| Total | 40 | 0 | 0 |

### 2. M.S.P. of Sun

| | M | D | H |
|---|---|---|---|
| Sun | 0 | 18 | 0 |
| Moon | 1 | 0 | 0 |
| Mars | 0 | 21 | 0 |
| Rahu | 1 | 24 | 0 |
| Jupiter | 1 | 18 | 0 |
| Saturn | 1 | 27 | 0 |
| Mercury | 1 | 21 | 0 |
| Ketu | 0 | 21 | 0 |
| Venus | 2 | 0 | 0 |
| Total | 12 | 0 | 0 |

### 3. M.S.P. of Moon

| | M | D | H |
|---|---|---|---|
| Moon | 1 | 20 | 0 |
| Mars | 1 | 5 | 0 |
| Rahu | 3 | 0 | 0 |
| Jupiter | 2 | 20 | 0 |
| Saturn | 3 | 5 | 0 |
| Mercury | 2 | 25 | 0 |
| Ketu | 1 | 5 | 0 |
| Venus | 3 | 10 | 0 |
| Sun | 1 | 0 | 0 |
| Total | 20 | 0 | 0 |

## 4. M.S.P. of Mars

| | M | D | H |
|---|---|---|---|
| Mars | 0 | 24 | 12 |
| Rahu | 2 | 3 | 0 |
| Jupiter | 1 | 26 | 0 |
| Saturn | 2 | 6 | 12 |
| Mercury | 1 | 29 | 12 |
| Ketu | 0 | 24 | 12 |
| Venus | 2 | 10 | 0 |
| Sun | 0 | 21 | 0 |
| Moon | 1 | 5 | 0 |
| **Total** | **14** | **0** | **0** |

## 5. M.S.P. of Rahu

| | M | D | H |
|---|---|---|---|
| Rahu | 5 | 12 | 0 |
| Jupiter | 4 | 24 | 0 |
| Saturn | 5 | 21 | 0 |
| Mercury | 5 | 3 | 0 |
| Ketu | 2 | 3 | 0 |
| Venus | 6 | 0 | 0 |
| Sun | 1 | 24 | 0 |
| Moon | 3 | 0 | 0 |
| Mars | 2 | 3 | 0 |
| **Total** | **36** | **0** | **0** |

## 6. M.S.P. of Jupiter

| | M | D | H |
|---|---|---|---|
| Jupiter | 4 | 8 | 0 |
| Saturn | 5 | 2 | 0 |
| Mercury | 4 | 16 | 0 |
| Ketu | 1 | 26 | 0 |
| Venus | 5 | 10 | 0 |
| Sun | 1 | 18 | 0 |
| Moon | 2 | 20 | 0 |
| Mars | 1 | 26 | 0 |
| Rahu | 4 | 24 | 0 |
| **Total** | **32** | **0** | **0** |

## 7. M.S.P. of Saturn

| | M | D | H |
|---|---|---|---|
| Saturn | 6 | 0 | 12 |
| Mercury | 5 | 11 | 12 |
| Ketu | 2 | 6 | 12 |
| Venus | 6 | 10 | 0 |
| Sun | 1 | 27 | 0 |
| Moon | 3 | 5 | 0 |
| Mars | 2 | 6 | 12 |
| Rahu | 5 | 21 | 0 |
| Jupiter | 5 | 2 | 0 |
| **Total** | **38** | **0** | **0** |

## 8. M.S.P. of Mercury

| | M | D | H |
|---|---|---|---|
| Mercury | 4 | 24 | 12 |
| Ketu | 1 | 29 | 12 |
| Venus | 5 | 20 | 0 |
| Sun | 1 | 21 | 0 |
| Moon | 2 | 25 | 0 |
| Mars | 1 | 29 | 12 |
| Rahu | 5 | 3 | 0 |
| Jupiter | 4 | 16 | 0 |
| Saturn | 5 | 11 | 12 |
| **Total** | **34** | **0** | **0** |

## 9. M.S.P. of Ketu

| | M | D | H |
|---|---|---|---|
| Ketu | 0 | 21 | 12 |
| Venus | 2 | 10 | 0 |
| Sun | 0 | 21 | 0 |
| Moon | 1 | 5 | 0 |
| Mars | 0 | 24 | 12 |
| Rahu | 2 | 3 | 0 |
| Jupiter | 1 | 26 | 0 |
| Saturn | 2 | 6 | 12 |
| Mercury | 1 | 29 | 12 |
| **Total** | **11** | **0** | **0** |

# Transit Dasha

We have already mentions before that transit means the temporary effect of the planets upon the native. This Dasha is called 'Gochara' in Sanskrit.

The house of the moon at birth is taken as the first house, and the transits of the various planets is calculated from that starting point. In Indian Astrology the moon sign is commonly referred to as "Janma Rashi", while in the Western System, it is known as the "Radical Moon". And the positions of the various planets at the time of transit are known as the "Transisting Sun", "Transiting Moon", "Transiting Mercury" and so on, in the Indian system of Astrology as well as the Western system of Astrology.

Suppose a person has the moon in Gemini in the horoscope at the time of birth, and on the day he consults the Astrologer the Moon is in Sagittarius, then we say that the transiting moon is the seventh from the Janma Rashi.

When a particular planet transits some places from the Janma Rashi, and if another planet is transiting a sensitive areas, the effects of the former's transit are obstructed. These sensitive areas— obstructing places—are known as "Vedha" in Sanskrit.

The effects of the transits of the planets in the twelve different houses, counted from the Janma Rashi at birth, may be grouped as follows:

# Sun's Transit

*First House* : Illness, sorrow, decline of prosperity, changes for the worse.

*Second House* : Decline in income, disappointments, diseases connected with the eye or head.

*Third House* : Good health, increase in income, promotion in job.

*Fourth House* : Loss of health, general unhappiness in the family, delay in undertakings.

*Fifth House* : Ill health, worries, persecution.

| | |
|---|---|
| *Sixth House* | : Increased income, contentment, improvement in general living conditions, good health, success in all undertakings. |
| *Seventh House* | : Financial problems, illness, sudden changes. |
| *Eighth House* | : Sorrow, illness, accidents, misunderstandings, stomach troubles. |
| *Ninth House* | : Ill health, frustrations, worries, danger from enemies. |
| *Tenth House* | : Success in undertakings, friendship of great men and women. |
| *Eleventh House* | : Profits in business, good luck in gambling, good health and honour. |
| *Twelfth House* | : Fever, worries and frustration, unnecessary wandering. |

Vedha places of Sun are :

3 and 9, 6 and 12, 10 and 4 and 11 and 5.

There is no Vedha between the Sun and Saturn as Sun is considered as the father of Saturn in the Astrological Mythology of the Hindus.

## Moon's Transit

The moon completes one orbit in 27 days. In other words he covers all the 12 signs in 27 days. Therefore, he is in each sign for approximately 2 days and 6 hours. The transits of moon has to be judged in terms of the sign he is passing through as counted from the Janma Rashi.

| | |
|---|---|
| *First House* | : Sound sleep, good food, gain of good clothes and ornaments. |
| *Second House* | : Unforeseen obstacles in undertakings, heavy expenditure, criticism from friends. |
| *Third House* | : Good health, success in all undertakings, unforeseen profits. |
| *Fourth House* | : Mental worries, unprofitable wandering. |
| *Fifth House* | : Disappointments, worries, sorrow, ill-health. |

| | |
|---|---|
| *Sixth House* | : Profits in business, success in all undertakings, good health, happiness in home life. |
| *Seventh House* | : Unforeseen luck, general happiness. |
| *Eighth House* | : Insomnia, worries, ill-health, losses in various ways, quarrels with friends. |
| *Ninth House* | : Fear from enemies, anxiety. |
| *Tenth House* | : Profits, success in undertakings. |
| *Eleventh House* | : Unexpected guests. |
| *Twelfth House* | : Heavy expenditure, anxiety |

Vedha places of Moon are :

1 and 5, 3 and 9, 6 and 12, 7 and 12, 10 and 4, 11 and 8.

There is no Vedha place between Moon and Mercury.

## Mar's Transit

| | |
|---|---|
| *First House* | : Fever, unnecessary travels, fear from enemies, anxieties. |
| *Second House* | : Obstacles, criticisms, heavy expenditure. |
| *Third House* | : Success in all undertakings, profits, good health. |
| *Fourth House* | : Aimless wandering, worries, ill health. |
| *Fifth House* | : Ill health, anxieties, disappointments, sorrow |
| *Sixth House* | : Happiness in home life, increase in assets, good health. |
| *Seventh House* | : Profits, general happiness. |
| *Eighth House* | : Ill-health, insomnia, worries, losses. |
| *Ninth House* | : Danger from enemies. |
| *Tenth House* | : Profits, success in all undertakings. |
| *Eleventh House* | : General happiness, success. |
| *Twelfth House* | : Heavy expenses, quarrels, criticisms. |

# Mercury's Transit

| | |
|---|---|
| *First House* | : Failure in examination, unhappy home life, forgetfulness. |
| *Second House* | : Increase in assets, unforeseen gains, good food, recognition of talents. |
| *Third House* | : Fear from foes, unhappy surroundings. |
| *Fourth House* | : General happiness in home life, increase in income. |
| *Fifth House* | : Quarrels with relatives, mental depression, sorrow. |
| *Sixth House* | : Success in all undertakings, gains through literary activities. |
| *Seventh House* | : Separation from family members and beloved ones, quarrels, general exhaustion. |
| *Eighth House* | : Success in all undertakings, general happiness. |
| *Ninth House* | : Quarrels with relatives, worries, ill-health. |
| *Tenth House* | : Increase in income, promotion in job, good health. |
| *Eleventh House* | : Profits in business, unforeseen luck. Happiness in family life. |
| *Twelfth House* | : Quarrels, illness, anxiety, humiliation. |

Vedha places of Mercury are :

2 and 5, 4 and 3, 6 and 9, 8 and 1, 10 and 7, 11 and 12.

# Jupiter's Transit

| | |
|---|---|
| *First House* | : Loss of position, anxiety, changes for the worse. |
| *Second House* | : Happiness in home life, gains from unexpected sources, success in undertakings. |
| *Third House* | : Danger from enemies. |
| *Fourth House* | : Death of close friends or relatives, heavy expenditure, general unhappiness. |

| | |
|---|---|
| *Fifth House* | : Great success in intellectual pursuits, honours, promotion in job, gains of clothes and jewels, increase in assets. |
| *Sixth House* | : Losses, ill-health, anxiety. |
| *Seventh House* | : Ill-health, mental worries. |
| *Eighth House* | : Illness in the family, unexpected tragedies, bondage, imprisonment, slander, unnecessary wanderings. |
| *Ninth House* | : Popularity, recognition of services, acts of charity. |
| *Tenth House* | : Losses, humiliation, obstacles. |
| *Eleventh House* | : Promotion increase in income unexpected gains. |
| *Twelfth House* | : Separation from spouse, heavy expenditure, despondency. |

Vedha places of Jupiter are :

2 and 12, 5 and 4, 7 and 3, 9 and 10, 11 and 18

## Venus's Transit

| | |
|---|---|
| *First House* | : Good food, sound sleep, comforts. |
| *Second House* | : Happiness in home life, increase in profits, honour. |
| *Third House* | : Unexpected gains, general happiness. |
| *Fourth House* | : Changes for the better, improvement in living conditions, honour of relatives, pleasant journeys. |
| *Fifth House* | : Happy home life, well being of family members. |
| *Sixth House* | : Illness to spouse, humiliations, anxiety. |
| *Seventh House* | : Quarrels with the opposite sex, tension, worries, minor illness. |
| *Eighth House* | : Expansion of landed properties, gains from unexpected sources, enjoyment with the opposite sex. |

| | |
|---|---|
| *Ninth House* | : Romance, profits, philanthropic activities. |
| *Tenth House* | : Disappointments, quarrels, humiliation, anxiety. |
| *Eleventh House* | : Happiness in home life, unexpected gains. |
| *Twelfth House* | : Gains in clothes and ornaments, perfumes, luxurious surroundings. |

Vedha places of Venus are :

1 and 8, 2 and 7, 3 and 1, 4 and 10, 5 and 9, 8 and 5, 9 and 11, 11 and 6, 12 and 13

## Saturn's Transit

| | |
|---|---|
| *First House* | : Illness to the spouse, children and relations, fear from enemies, petty quarrels, bad food, worries. |
| *Second House* | : Ill-health, losses, unnecessary wandering, quarrels, general unhappiness. |
| *Third House* | : Success in undertakings, gains, recognition of talents, happy events, good news. |
| *Fourth House* | : Ill-health in family, sorrow, worries. |
| *Fifth House* | : Losses of money and friends, insults, humiliation, illness, quarrels. |
| *Sixth House* | : Success in all undertakings, defeat of enemies, unexpected profits, good news. |
| *Seventh House* | : Separation from the spouse, journey, heavy expenses, minor illness. |
| *Eighth House* | : Litigation, public scandal, death of near relatives, general unhappiness. |
| *Ninth House* | : Decline in income, losses, misunderstandings. |
| *Tenth House* | : Illness, humiliation, unnecessary wanderings. |
| *Eleventh House* | : Recognition of merits, gains of riches, good news, expansion of assets. |
| *Twelfth House* | : Sorrow, heavy expenditure, accidents. |

Vedha places of Saturn are :

3 and 12, 6 and 9, 11 and 5.

There is no Vedha between Saturn and Sun.

Sun and Mars will usher in their effects as soon as they enter the houses, while Jupiter and Venus, half way in the houses, Saturn at the time of leaving the houses, and Moon and Mercury throughout their sojourn.

The guidelines of the effects provided above will be tempered by the strength or weakness by position, rulership and aspect of their planets. For example, besides the Vedha position, an aspect between a good and bad planet counterbalances the effects of both, whereas the bad aspect, of two bad planets will multiply the bad effects. Naturally, the good effects of a weak planet will be weak. However, the Moon just becomes the enhancer of the good or bad effects indicated by the various planets with which it conjoins during its temporary stay in the different houses.

Transit system, should always be considered with the Dasha system, checking one with the other. And it should be borne in mind that however benevolent a planet may be in its blessings, during its transit, the Dasha system also should lend itself to be taken advantage of. And also, while coming to the final analysis by this method, the value of all the planets in the various houses should be taken into account, and their new effect alone should be considered.

It is also essential to bear in mind that no two horoscopes are identical. Only the relative strengths of the various planets and special aptitudes in respect of individual horoscopes should be taken into account. And each reading should be individualised, with giving ample emphasis to the nature's innate nature while making prediction.

# CHAPTER THIRTEEN

# Glossary

**Affliction** : (*i*) When one planet is weak by being dehilited or in detriment it is said to be afflicted.

    (*ii*) (*a*) If a planet is conjoined with a malefic or parallel with a malefic planet or forming opposition, square or unfavourable aspect with a planet it is deemed to be afflicted.

    (*c*) If a planet is in square or opposition aspect with a benefic, then it is called afflicted.

**Note** : If a planet be weak, in detriment or in dehility and conjoined with a malefic and also forming direct or opposition aspect with a malefic the planet would be called much afflicted. If, however, there be only one of the above mentioned circumstances present and there be good aspects from strong benefics the affliction would stand considerably mitigated. Individual judgement must determine in each case the extent of affliction.

**Airy Signs** : Gemini, Libra and Aquarius are called Airy signs.

**Angles** : The ascendant, cusps of the 4th, 7th and 10th house are called Kendra or angles. The planets placed in the angles are considered more powerful than they are in other houses.

**Ascendant** : The point of the zodiac which touches the eastern horizon as viewed from the place of birth at the time of birth. This is also called rising sign or cusp of the time of 1st house. The sign which is present is 1st house is called ascendant.

**Aspects** : Planets are believed to east their 'aspect' or 'Drishathi'. Normally all planets aspect the planets placed 180° or seven houses apart. Only three planets. : Mars, Saturn and Jupiter also respectively aspect fourth, eighth; third and tenth and fifth and ninth houses from their position.

**Barren Signs** : Gemini, Leo, Virgo

**Benefics (Natural)** : Jupiter and Venus. Other planets also become benefic owing to their typical position and their relations, with the lagna lord.

**Bestial Signs** : The following signs are called bestial because their names pertain to beasts : Aries, Taurus, Leo, Sagittarius and Capricorn.

**Cardinal Signs** : Aries, Cancer, Libra, Capricorn.

**Combust** : When a planet comes with in 8.5° of the Sun, the planet loses part of its power and individual qualities because the ray emitted by it gets mixed and burnt up with Sun's rays. A combust planet is deemed weak.

**Common Signs** : Gemini, Virgo, Sagittarius, Pisces.

**Dehility** : A planet in a sign opposite to one it is an exaltation is deemed to be in dehility.

**Detriment** : If a planet is in a sign opposites to one, its owns it is deemed to be in detriment. Like these Sun in Aquarius, Moon in Capricorn, Mars in Libra or Taurus, Mercury in Sagittarius or Pisces, Jupiter in Gemini, or Virgo, Venus in Aries or Scorpio, Saturn in Cancer or Leo are deemed to be in detriment. This is, thus, a weak position.

**Direct Motion** : When a planet is moving forward it is in direct motion. The Sun and Moon have only direct motion while others have backward or retrograde motion too. Rahu and Ketu always move in retrograde direction.

**Dispositor** : The lord of the sign in which a planet is. Suppose the Moon is in Taurus. Then Venus is the dispositor of Moon. Suppose the Moon is in Gemini, then Mercury is the dispositor of the Moon.

**Earth Signs** : Taurus, Virgo and Capricorn are earth signs.

**Exaltation** : As mentioned in the 2nd Chapter, each planet has a sign wherein it shows its qualities best. That sign is called the 'Usheha

Rashi' or the exaltation sign for that planet. Likes the Sun gets exalted in Aries, Moon in Taurus and so on. Exaltation is the position of maximum strength.

**Faminine Sings** : Taurus, Cancer, Virgo, Scorpio, Capricorn, Pisces.

**Fiery Signs** : Aries, Leo, Sagittarius are called fiery signs.

**Fixed Signs** : Taurus, Leo, Scorpio, Aquarius.

**Fruitful Signs** : Cancer, Scorpio, Pisces.

**Human Signs** : Gemini, Virgo, Aquarius and first 15° of Sagittarius.

**Lights or Luminaries** : The Sun and the Moon.

**Local Time or Local Mean Time** : This is reckoned as follows.

Suppose the place of birth is India (where the Indian Standard Time IST) has been fixed on the basis of 82°30′ of longitude east of Greenwich) and the IST is 4 p.m. What would be the local mean time at a city in India with longitude 70 ? Deducting 70° from 82′ 30′ we get 12°30′. At the rate of 4 minutes for each degree and 4 seconds for each minutes of arc, we get 50 minutes, deducting 50 minutes from 4 p.m. We get 3.10 p.m. This would be local mean time.

**Lords** : The ruler (of a sign or the house)

**Malefics** (Natural) : Mars and Saturn (Also reckon Rahu and Ketu).

**Masculine Signs** : Aries, Gemini, Leo, Libra, Sagittarius, Aquarius.

**Mutable Signs** : Gemini, Virgo, Sagittarius, Pisces.

**Nativity** : Horoscope or birth chart giving position of planets, rising signs or ascendants and cusp of Houses.

**Northern Signs** : Aries, Taurus, Gemini, Cancer, Leo and Virgo.

**Own House** : The Sign in the house or houses owned by the particular planets. Like if Leo be in 4th house, the 4th house gets ruled by Sun. In case the planet be the ruler of the two signs viz Mercury ruling over Gemini and Virgo, — in that case if the signs be in 9th or 12th house Mercury becomes the ruler of these houses.

**Retrograde** : The backward motion which the planets appear to have at times, on account of the position and motion of earth.

**Rising Sign** : The ascendant or sign in which the cusp of the 1st house is.

**Ruler** : See lords.

**Ruling Planet** : Ruler of the ascendant is called the ruling planet.

**Sidereal Time** : Angular distance of the first point of Aries.

**Signs** : Twelve parts of the zodiac each comprising 30°, the signs in order are Aries, Taurus, Gemini, Cancer, Leo, Virgo, Libra, Scorpio, Sagittarius, Capricorn, Aquarius and Pisces.

**Southern Signs** : Libra, Scorpio, Sagittarius, Capricorn, Aquarius, Pisces.

**Standard Time** : Times by which the watch prevalent in a particular country. The IST is 5 hours 30 minutes ahead of GMT. This is since 1903, before that, Madras time was the IST of India. In the ancient India, the 0° longitude was believed to be in Ujjain (the Mahakal Temple) according to which time was reckoned then like now it is Greenwich Lab in England.

**Succedent Houses** : The 2nd, 5th, 8th and 11th houses.

**Transit** : The passage of any planet over radical place of any planet (normally the moon sign in the natal chart), cusps of 1st, 4th, 7th or 10th house or over any sensitive point.

**Trikona House** : The houses 5th and 9th. Placement of any planet in these add power to these planets which are deemed to get maximum power when in the Kendra (Angles) houses (1st, 4th, 7th, 10th).

**Tropical Signs** : Cancer, Capricorn.

**Watery Signs** : Cancer, Scorpio, Pisces.

**Zodiac** : The imaginary path around the earth through which the Sun appears to travel. Also called ecliptic.

# NOTES